Writing Models

Year 5

Other titles of interest:

Writing Models Year 3
Pie Corbett
ISBN 1-84312-094-1

Writing Models Year 4
Pie Corbett
ISBN 1-84312-095-X

Writing Models Year 6
Pie Corbett
ISBN 1-84312-097-6

Jumpstart!
Key Stage 2/3 Literacy Games
Pie Corbett
ISBN 1-84312-102-6

Word Power
Activities for Years 3 and 4
Terry Saunders
ISBN 1-84312-141-7

Word Power
Activities for Years 5 and 6
Terry Saunders
ISBN 1-84312-142-5

Writing Models

Year 5

Pie Corbett

 **David Fulton** Publishers

David Fulton Publishers Ltd
The Chiswick Centre, 414 Chiswick High Road, London W4 5TF

www.fultonpublishers.co.uk

First published in 2004 in Great Britain by David Fulton Publishers

10 9 8 7 6 5 4 3 2 1

David Fulton Publishers is a division of ITV plc.

Note: The right of Pie Corbett to be identified as the author of this work has been asserted by him
in accordance with the Copyright, Designs and Patents Act 1988.

Copyright © Pie Corbett 2004

British Library Cataloguing in Publication Data
A catalogue record for this book is available from the British Library.

ISBN 1-84312-096-8

Designed and typeset by Kenneth Burnley, Wirral, Cheshire
Printed and bound in Great Britain

Contents

Introduction

What does the book contain?

This is part of a series of books for use at Key Stage 2 that contain banks of photocopiable models for writing, covering the full writing range of poetry, fiction and non-fiction for pupils in Years 3–6.

For each text type a complete example has been provided. For some text types, there is also a supplementary extract focusing on a specific aspect of the text type, e.g. openings. Annotated copies of simpler examples provide key teaching points at a glance. There are also simple teachers' notes that give a swift outline of reading and writing activities linked to the examples. To help with differentiation we have included simpler and harder examples.

How to use the model texts to teach writing

Writing begins with reading. The more familiar children are with a text type, the more likely it is that they will be able to write in a similar vein. This is because children who read avidly will have internalised the patterns of language. When they come to write, they can then easily slip into the right 'voice' so that what they write 'sounds right'. It is not surprising that the best writers in a class are always children who read. So, any work on writing will always begin with reading plenty of examples.

You also need to provide plenty of opportunities to 'talk the text type', using the same sort of language. For instance, when working on narrative, story-telling helps many children to begin using the appropriate patterns of narrative language. If you are teaching them how to write recounts, then telling anecdotes will get the children into the 'right' voice.

Written text types	Oral text types
Narrative	Story-telling
Poetry	Poetry performance
Recount	Anecdotes
Explanation	Explaining
Report	Informing
Discussion	Debates
Persuasion	Arguing a viewpoint

Ideally, it helps if you can set up something interesting and motivating as a starting point for writing. This may involve first-hand experience, drama, video, music, art, a visit, and so on. Children will be more committed to writing if there is a purpose and some sort of genuine audience. Therefore it helps to publish writing through display, the school website, booklets, photocopied anthologies, etc.

Introduction

How to use this book

The models in this book can be turned into OHTs, or photocopied, to use in a variety of ways:

1 Analysis

Either as a whole class, in pairs or as individuals, encourage the children to read the text as writers and analyse the structure and language features.

To prepare for writing, look at the specific models provided in this book, analysing how they are structured and what language features are used. The annotated versions and teachers' notes will draw your attention to these. Try to avoid the temptation to tell the children but let them annotate the examples and work out as much as they can for themselves. A problem-solving approach is more likely to embed the learning! This analysis can be turned into a 'writer's toolkit' – a reminder sheet or wall chart that can be used during writing and referred to afterwards for self-evaluation and marking.

Before launching into writing, you may feel that the class needs to practise the spelling of certain key words. For instance, when working on traditional tales, learning how to spell 'once' would be handy! Furthermore, certain specific sentence structures might be needed for the text type you are working on, and these too could be rehearsed. For instance, you could try practising putting together opening lines, or writing sentences beginning 'Suddenly . . .', and so forth. These can be practised on mini-whiteboards. To find ideas for sentence and spelling games, see my book *Jumpstart!*, available from David Fulton.

2 Demonstration

You can use the models in this book to demonstrate how to write each of the text types. In the NLS video *Grammar for Writing* you can see teachers holding models in their hands or glancing at a model pinned up beside the board. While writing they talk through their decisions, rehearsing sentences, making alterations and rereading to check for sense and accuracy. When demonstrating, try to ensure that you make specific reference back to the models and the writer's toolkit. Demonstration is useful for any aspect of writing that is new, or that children find difficult. In demonstration, you are able directly to explain and show pupils how to write a text type.

3 Shared writing

Demonstration is usually followed by shared composition. Here, you act as scribe for the class or group, leaving them free to focus on the composition. This does not mean accepting any old contribution, but pushing the class to think for themselves and to evaluate their ideas. Weak vocabulary and sentence structure should be challenged. The class may need reminding to return to the model or check the writer's toolkit. In shared composition the teacher scaffolds the pupils' attempts. If children struggle with their own writing, then you will need to keep returning to shared writing, gradually handing over more and more of the decisions to the class.

4 Independent writing

Shared writing is usually followed by independent writing. Some children will still find it helpful to have a model to hand for reference as they write. Certainly the model, and the writer's toolkit, can be used for self-evaluation and marking. Some children may need extra support during shared writing – this might be through working with an adult, a partner, using a writing frame, a bank of vocabulary or sentence starters. However, the aim is for the majority to be able to write independently.

Guided writing can be used to teach at the point of writing – to support and challenge. If you find you are stretched for time, it may be more important to use guided time to focus on those who struggle. This means that class teaching can be aimed high.

5 Evaluation

After writing, children can self-evaluate. This might be carried out in pairs by using response partners. The author should read through his or her own writing, identifying strengths. He or she can then make selected improvements to the composition – as well as checking on accuracy.

If you are marking the work, try to keep your comments focused, indicating what has worked well and where improvements need to be made:

- Use a highlighter to highlight the best parts.
- Indicate where improvements are needed using symbols such as dotted lines, etc.

When work is returned, pupils should read what the teacher has written, sign it and then be given an opportunity to respond. There should be a range of improvements that each child can make, for example using a more powerful word, improving sentence structure, adding in more information, dropping in a clause, correcting punctuation, improving common spellings, etc. Your marking will also lead the following sessions as it should identify what has to be taught next.

Using technology

It can be helpful if several children write straight onto blank OHTs. This means that in the plenary, or the next day, these can be used for whole-class teaching – identifying strengths, checking against the models and toolkits and showing how to improve. If you have an interactive whiteboard then a child can compose straight onto the screen. I find it useful if the author will come out, read their own work through and explain what they are pleased with and discuss areas that might need further work. This evidently calls for some sensitive handling, though in the main most children enjoy their chance at the OHP!

Introduction

Why use a model?

Sometimes the reading material we use provides an ideal model. For instance, Kit Wright's poem 'Magic Box' works without fail to produce good quality writing. However, most adult writing for children is actually too subtle and complex to offer a model that can easily be imitated. To put it bluntly, Betsy Byars's *The Midnight Fox* may be a great book to use with Year 5 children. But she is a remarkable writer working at level 3,000, and Darren aged $9^3/_4$ years is only at level 2! So, the specific models in this book provide clear structures that will support children's own writing. Those who struggle as writers should stick to imitating the models – while your most able pupils will have already internalised the patterns and should not be hindered from moving beyond.

Poetry models

A List of Small and Happy Things

How happy –
when you take
that first bite
of a chocolate ice
and shudder.

How happy –
when you discover
another sweet in your pocket
even though it's covered
in fluff!

How happy –
when you shout
and your echo
boomerangs back.

How happy –
when you see
a six-spot ladybird crawl
up a blade of grass.

How happy –
when you run
so fast that the wind
catches your breath.

How happy –
when you discover
how to pat your head
and rub your tummy
at the same time.

Pie Corbett

TERM 1: **POEMS CONVEYING FEELINGS, MOODS OR REFLECTIONS**
(Easier)

A List of
Small and Happy Things

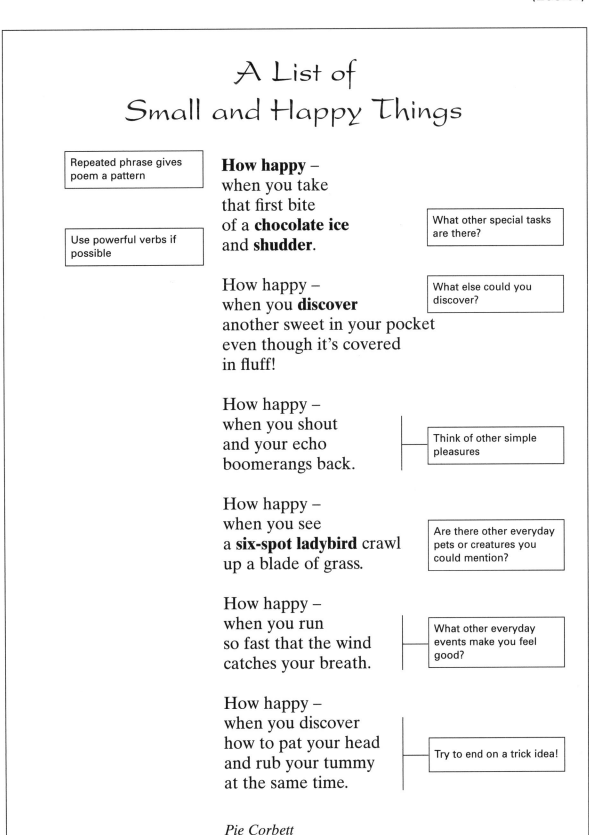

Repeated phrase gives poem a pattern

How happy –
when you take
that first bite
of a **chocolate ice**
and **shudder**.

What other special tasks are there?

Use powerful verbs if possible

How happy –
when you **discover**
another sweet in your pocket
even though it's covered
in fluff!

What else could you discover?

How happy –
when you shout
and your echo
boomerangs back.

Think of other simple pleasures

How happy –
when you see
a **six-spot ladybird** crawl
up a blade of grass.

Are there other everyday pets or creatures you could mention?

How happy –
when you run
so fast that the wind
catches your breath.

What other everyday events make you feel good?

How happy –
when you discover
how to pat your head
and rub your tummy
at the same time.

Try to end on a trick idea!

Pie Corbett

Autobiography

1. Living at the end of the terrace,
   two up, two down –
   with the bus-stop outside the bedroom window.
   Sitting in the metal tub in the backyard with my brothers –
   or warm in winter in front of the stove.
   Mum tugging the bucket up from the village well.

2. Standing in the playground
   at my first school – quite lost.
   So many big children – not knowing what to do or where to go.

3. Assembly.
   Sitting on the shiny wooden floor staring at the cracks.
   Singing hymns and having to mouth the words aloud.
   Watching clouds drift by the jam-jars on the classroom window.
   Bringing in a bunch of daffodils, the stems crunched together.
   Watching tadpoles spin round in the class goldfish bowl.
   Filling my best friend Petie's wellington boots with frogspawn.

4. Falling off the back of a van.
   Feeling my leg snap and waiting, twisted on the ground
   while it backs towards me, over me.
   Smelling the hot darkness beneath the van
   as my brothers screamed.

5. Moving from the village
   to the farm.
   It smelt strange.
   Sunlight waking me every morning.
   My cat, found one winter in the snow,
   curled asleep like a question mark in the barn.

TERM 1: **POEMS CONVEYING FEELINGS, MOODS OR REFLECTIONS**
(Harder)

6. Petie and I took to the stage, dressed as a blue elephant.
    Playing the piano with two fingers, learning lists of Latin verbs –
    I can still stay 'I love you' so I'm well equipped,
    if I get whipped back in time.
    Playing rugby when the ground was harder than iron;
    swimming in the rain,
    colouring in the Pyramids and Henry the Eighth.
    Drawing battle plans in my history book,
    playing cricket in the yard.
    Swapping cigarette cards, collecting *The Man from Uncle*
    and later, 'James Bond'; writing to Big Chief Eye Spy –
    a signed-up member of the Dan Dare Club,
    complete with red cellophane X-ray specs.

7. Running across the fields with Hamlet,
    a spotty dog we fetched back from the pound.
    Throwing stones at rats, cleaning out the pigs.
    Apples and pears; late-night frost pots
    glowing in the dark; as if the fields were on fire.

8. Holidays
    at Camber Sands – waves wrinkling the sea.
    Walking with no shoes on.
    Late-night fish and chips, salt and vinegar tang.
    Dad laughing – remembering his laugh
    that is now silent.

    Pie Corbett

Images List

Windows:
glass eyes;
open mouths.

Pillows:
soft Weetabix;
purse of dreams.

Fingernails:
jagged moons;
suns rising.

Flames:
hot lips;
living leaves.

Leaves:
frail maps;
lost starfish.

Lightning:
hair-thin cracks in a vase;
a heart attack strokes the dark.

TERM 1: **POEMS USING METAPHORS AND SIMILIES**
(Easier)

Images List

State a subject

Windows:
glass eyes;
open mouths.

Think of comparisons

Pillows:
soft Weetabix;
purse of dreams.

Notice pattern and punctuation

Why a purse?

Fingernails:
jagged moons;
suns rising.

These ideas are visual

Flames:
hot lips;
living leaves.

Alliteration

Leaves:
frail **maps**;
lost starfish.

In what way is a leaf like a map?

Why 'lost'?

Lightning:
hair-thin **cracks** in a vase;
a heart attack **strokes** the dark.

Play on words – it could be a verb or a noun

Why do you think the poet chose this word?

Taking One Idea for a Walk

Windows

Glass eyes glare
in the morning sun
across city lawns,
watching traffic snarl
on the High Street,
and neat flower beds
where tulips bloom
and old folk sit,
feeding pigeons.

Glass eyes stare
at shop windows,
at cats sneaking
a peek into dustbins,
at dogs fast asleep
in back yards,
at the distant hills
and clouds flowering
the so blue sky.

Glass eyes gaze
at the weary maze
of the city at dusk;
peering down
at the blossom
of streetlights.

Poetry models

Glass eyes
shut tight,
as night
steals day
light.

Pie Corbett

The Blue Elephant

Everyone was excited,
our class was putting on a play.
It was going to be a mystery –
complete with robbers, detectives
and a heroine . . .

'Today, we choose the parts,'
explained Mr Weedler, Head Teacher
and chief misery in my life:
beater of boys and stoker of boilers.

Petie and I fancied ourselves as the detectives,
so we stuck up our hands
as high as we could reach
and made eager noises,
grunting and waggling our fingers
for all we were worth.

But the Harrison twins got the best parts.
We should have guessed –
always smartly dressed,
with their brilliant hair,
Brylcreemed back
in a tidal slick.

Petie and I ended up as the elephant.
The Blue Elephant.
I was the back end –
hot beneath the lights,
arms tight round Petie's waist.
I waited, frightened, in the dark,
hoping Petie could see his way
across the stage, for the eyeslits
were cut thin to make it look mean.

The Blue Elephant

Everyone was excited,
our class was putting on a play.
It was going to be a mystery –
complete with robbers, detectives
and a heroine . . .

> Use an anecdotal voice

'Today, we choose the parts,'
explained **Mr Weedler**, Head Teacher
and chief misery in my life:
beater of **b**oys and stoker of **b**oilers.

> Use names

> Use of alliteration for emphasis

Petie and I fancied ourselves as the detectives,
so we stuck up our hands
as high as we could reach
and made eager noises,
grunting and waggling our fingers
for all we were worth.

> Show how people feel through what they do

But the Harrison twins got the best parts.
We should have gu**essed** –
always smartly dr**essed**,
with their **b**rilliant hair,
Brylcreemed **back**
in a tidal sli**ck**.

> Rhyme used to show how 'slick' they were!

> Repeated end sounds

> Alliteration

Petie and I ended up as the elephant.
The Blue Elephant.
I was the back end –
hot beneath the lights,
arms tight round Petie's waist.
I waited, **frightened**, in the dark,
hoping Petie could see his way
across the stage, for the eyeslits
were cut thin to make it look **mean**.

> Use details

> Explain how you felt

> Use a little description to paint a scene

Then we were on,
trunk wagging,
feet stomping.
But halfway across
Petie lost it –
tripped and down we went,
with a crash that would have woken Hollywood –
taking with us the side wall
of the cardboard police station.

The audience roared,
and later, my father declared
the whole play a great success.

But the Harrison twins
never spoke to Petie or me again,
for we had ruined their dramatic entry.

And all I remember now
was the nervous beating of my heart
so hard that I could feel its pulse.
It seemed to be stuck in my throat.

And I lay on the ground,
knowing that I'd made a fool of myself again
and that Mr Weedler's wrath
would know no bounds this time.
For here was a man who
beat us for our own good.

So these many years later,
I hope never to trip again,
nervous in the dark,
unable to see
the next step ahead.

Pie Corbett

Poetry models

Then we were on,
trunk **wagging**,
feet **stomping**.
But halfway across
Petie lost it –
tripped and down we went,
with a crash that would have woken Hollywood –
taking with us the side wall
of the cardboard police station.

Use power-ful verbs where possible

The audience **roared**,
and later, my father declared
the whole play a great success.

Use 'But' at the start of a sentence for emphasis

But the Harrison twins
never spoke to Petie or me again,
for we had ruined their dramatic entry.

And all I remember now
was the nervous beating of my heart
so hard that I could feel its pulse.
It seemed to be stuck in my throat.

Explain feelings

And I lay on the ground,
knowing that I'd made a fool of myself again
and that Mr Weedler's wrath
would know no bounds this time.
For here was a man who
beat us for our own good.

So these many years later,
I hope never to trip again,
nervous in the dark,
unable to see
the next step ahead.

End with a comment on the events

Pie Corbett

Left Behind

The unicorns were left off the ark
for making unpleasant remarks
about the dinosaurs taking up too much room –

and besides, Mrs Noah thought their horns
looked far too scary.

The dragons were considered
a fire hazard –
and the dwarves turned up late.

The Minotaur roared too loudly,
would have kept everyone awake –

Pegasus got in a flap
and Medusa could not produce a
look, without freezing the others to stone.

The Trolls kept bickering
and the giants were banned
because they bullied the buffalo
and made the bison weep.

The fairies managed to sneak in,
tucked beneath an elephant's ear

and spent the whole journey
hiding in the ship's rafters,
spreading laughter amongst the sheep.

The angels quarrelled with the gnomes
and ran the risk of being left at home.

So, as the ark slipped over the horizon,
a small band of creatures was left behind.

Till at the last minute, as the storm broke,
the storytellers' voices spoke

and a second ark appeared.

Pie Corbett

Mysteries

Why do dogs bury bones?
Why do kids like mobile phones?
Why do cats knead their paws?
Why does grass grow out of doors?

Why do clouds disappear?
Why do dads drink lukewarm beer?
Why do birds sing at dawn?
Why do babies get stillborn?

Why do stars shine at night?
Why is maths always right?
Why do toes grow so slow?
Why avoid the mistletoe?

Why do stories have to end?
Why do cuts always mend?
Why do plums have a stone?
Why do tramps stay on their own?

Why do bombers want to kill?
Why does fame cause such a thrill?
Why do measles make us ill?
Why does time not keep still?

Why do robbers grab and smash?
Why do nappies cause a rash?
Why do mysteries mystify?
Are the answers camera shy?

Pie Corbett

Poetry models

Mysteries

Play on words
(knead/need)

Why do dogs bury bones?
Why do kids like mobile phones?
Why do cats **knead** their paws?
Why does grass grow out of doors?

Try answering some of
these questions!

Use mystifying
questions!

Why do clouds disappear?
Why do dads drink lukewarm beer?
Why do birds sing at dawn?
Why do babies get stillborn?

Contrast sad/happy ideas
for impact

You can break the
pattern

Why do stars shine at night?
Why **is** maths always right?
Why do toes grow so slow?
Why **avoid** the mistletoe?

Why do stories have to end?
Why do cuts always mend?
Why do plums have a stone?
Why do tramps stay on their own?

Rhyming couplets

Why do bombers want to kill?
Why does fame cause such a thrill?
Why do measles make us ill?
Why does time not keep still?

Tap out the rhythm – or say
sentences aloud so they
match each other

Transposed
phrase

Why do robbers **grab and smash**?
Why do nappies cause a rash?
Why do mysteries mystify?
Are the answers camera shy?

Try to find a simple way to
end

Pie Corbett

Cool!

Somebody said that
my new jeans were cool!
But I've never seen them shivering,
even when they're alone in the cupboard.

Somebody said
that my new haircut was cool!
But I never noticed
a layer of frost on my hair.

Somebody said
that my Man. United strip was cool!
But actually it's quite cosy
and keeps me hot under the collar.

Somebody said
that eating chilli was cool!
But as far as I'm concerned
it's hotter than pure pepper.

Somebody said
that the latest dance was cool!
Well, I'm no fool
because the way I dance is dead hot!

Somebody said
that the latest song
by some boy band was cool!
But to me it was just hot air.

Somebody said
that bunking off school was cool!
But as far as I can tell
it just gets you into hot water.

Somebody said
that ice cream was cool!
And being no fool,
I had to agree.

Pie Corbett

Fiction models

1. The bomb exploded.

2. 'Jump!' yelled Shan.

3. Inside the old house, it was dusty and dark.

4. 'What was that?' The two girls stared up the lane, peering into the alley.

5. Although the afternoon sun was still warm, Jazzy felt cold. Cold to the bone. She shuddered.

6. 'Don't talk to old Warder,' said Mr Pender for what seemed like the hundredth time. 'You know he's not to be trusted.'

7. Sian turned and began to run as hard and as fast as she could.

8. 'When does the bus get here?' asked Simone, turning to Brad. He shook his head and shrugged his shoulders.

Fiction models

Dramatic opening using a short sentence	1. The bomb exploded.
Exclamation opening	2. **'Jump!'** yelled Shan.
Open with 'Inside' or 'Outside' plus description	3. **Inside** the old house, it was **d**usty and **d**ark.
Question opening	4. **'What was that?'** The two girls **stared** up the lane, **peering** into the alley.
Contrasting opening using 'Although'	5. **Although** the afternoon sun was still warm, Jazzy felt **cold**. **Cold** to the bone. She **shuddered**.
Warning opening	6. **'Don't talk to old Warder,'** said Mr Pender for what seemed like the hundredth time. 'You know he's not to be trusted.'
Open with a character's name	7. **Sian** turned and began to run as hard and as fast as she could.
Question opening / Add an '-ing' clause to show what the speaker is doing	8. **'When does the bus get here?'** asked Simone, **turning** to Brad. He **sh**ook his head and **sh**rugged his **sh**oulders.

Annotations (right margin):
- (3) Alliteration to make line memorable
- (4) Verbs suggest the girls are nervous
- (5) Repetition of 'cold' for emphasis
- (5) Verb reinforces cold but suggests fear
- (7) Dramatic action in opening
- (8) Alliteration makes the line more memorable

TERM 1: **STORY OPENINGS – ACTION, DESCRIPTION, DIALOGUE**
(Harder)

1. The Rottweiler growled, stood up and began to move towards the children. They stared into its red eyes and knew that it was only a moment away from leaping . . .

2. 'Watch out!' yelled Kria, grabbing hold of Tim's arm as a spear landed with a thud into the damp earth. They stared up, and standing at the top of the pit was what looked like an ancient Briton . . .

3. The door to the house was ajar as if inviting them in. Inside, it was so dark that at first they could not make out the piles of broken furniture, the dusty floorboards and the two large sacks of money.

4. 'Have you ever been into the old abattoir?' asked Jenny, turning to her friend. 'No way!' replied Kirsty, 'not only would it be really spooky but just think of all the dust!' She smoothed her school skirt. It was new and her mum had not really been able to afford it.

5. A thick mist crept down the lane, smothering the gardens, cutting out the daylight. Jem stood on the path and began to feel alone. It was as if the mist had crept around him like a living creature . . .

6. 'Don't you dare go down to the canal,' snapped Mrs Jarvis. The two boys grinned behind her back. 'Of course not,' replied Connor, trying to sound innocent.

TERM 1: **STORY OPENINGS – ACTION, DESCRIPTION, DIALOGUE**
(Harder)

7. Brad clenched his fist as tight as a stone and waited. They would be coming down the path any moment now . . .

8. 'What is that?' asked Jan, staring down into the water. Billy crouched down, adjusted his glasses and squinted.

TERM 1: **CHARACTERISATION – ACTION, DESCRIPTION, DIALOGUE**
(Easier)

1. As soon as he saw Kyle, Trev's face creased into a smile. He picked up his leather jacket and dashed over the road.

2. Bravely, Macshane plunged his hand into the hot water and picked up the precious ring. His hand was red and blisters began to appear.

3. Courtney marched into the classroom, slung her bag down and began to chat loudly. Everyone gathered around.

4. Gardiner thought about old Mrs Glew. She lived all alone on the estate and no one ever visited her. Now he felt bad about what he had done.

5. 'Leave me alone!' snarled Trev, turning his back on Courtney.

6. Courtney shoved her homework into her bag. She stared at Trev. She wondered what had brought on this sudden change of mood.

7. 'He's angry about being given detention,' suggested Jess calmly.

8. Macshane looked carefully at Trev. He was in an awful state. His hair was like a bird's nest, his jeans torn and he had lost one shoe. What had happened?

9. 'Hi,' said Gabbler quietly, helping his friend off the ground. 'Thanks,' muttered Trev.

Fiction models

1. As soon as he saw Kyle, Trev's face **creased** into a smile. He picked up his **leather** jacket and **dashed** over the road.

   | Reaction |

   | Detail |

   | Powerful verb suggests he is pleased |

2. **Bravely**, Macshane plunged his hand into the hot water and picked up the precious ring. **His hand was red and blisters began to appear.**

   | Adverb starter tells how he feels |

   | Shows how brave he was |

3. Courtney **marched** into the classroom, **slung** her bag down and began to **chat loudly**. **Everyone gathered around.**

   | Use verbs and adverbs to suggest character |

   | Reactions of bystanders |

4. Gardiner thought about old Mrs Glew. She lived all alone on the estate and no one ever visited her. Now he felt bad about what he had done.

   | Reveal a character's thoughts |

5. 'Leave me alone!' **snarled** Trev, **turning his back on Courtney.**

   | Speech verb to show character |

   | 'ing' clause to show what he does as he speaks |

6. Courtney shoved her homework into her bag. She stared at Trev. She **wondered what had brought on this sudden change of mood.**

   | Reveal what another character thinks |

7. **'He's angry about being given detention,'** suggested Jess calmly.

   | Use another character's views |

8. Macshane looked carefully at Trev. He was in an awful state. His hair was like a bird's nest, his jeans torn and he had lost one shoe. **What had happened?**

   | Have another character describe the main character |

   | Use a question to make the reader think |

9. 'Hi,' said Gabbler **quietly, helping his friend off the ground.** 'Thanks,' **muttered** Trev.

   | Use speech verbs or an adverb to indicate feelings |

   | Add in a supporting action |

TERM 1: CHARACTERISATION – ACTION, DESCRIPTION, DIALOGUE
(Harder)

---

1. Ferret spun round and grinned. His two front teeth flashed gold.

2. Kate grabbed the blazing torch and held it up high, even though it was dangerous. Although no one was listening, she let out a sudden yell.

3. Petie Fisher strode down to the chip shop. His new sneakers creaked as he walked, the leather biting into his feet.

4. Carson thought about his mother. It was time to visit her. He didn't visit her enough. She knew so many things and he knew so little. It was time that he found out the truth about his past.

5. 'Gerroff!' yelled Carson, spitting the words out like gunfire.

6. Tina stopped tying the parcel up. She glared back at Carson. Not for the first time did she heave an inward sigh. He was so difficult, so moody. She wondered what had caused such deep unease.

7. 'She's jealous, that's what I think,' replied Jess cautiously.

8. Petie glanced slyly at Carson from the corner of his eye. No one dared to look at him straight on. Rather look a rattler in the eye. He noticed the locket, swinging at his neck. It seemed out of place and Petie wondered whose photo it contained.

---

9. 'Hello,' said Gabbler, grabbing the dog's lead with one hand and the ice cream with the other. Tim gave a sudden grin of warmth. He picked up his skateboard, tucked it under his arm and wandered over to his friend. 'Hi'ya,' mumbled Tim.

One afternoon my mother asked me to go and fetch my father in from ploughing the old field under Samson Hill.

I made my way down to the shore. Standing there, I listened to the waves rolling on the beach. The sun beat down and I could feel the sand under my feet. I sat down and tugged off my socks. I tied my laces together, slung my shoes over my shoulder and walked along the shore. The sand felt warm and soft under my bare feet. Only the shells dug into my skin.

Well before Rushy Bay, I stopped. I could hear the distant sound of the old tractor rumbling its way up and down the field. So, I put my shoes back on and made my way towards Samson Hill. I could feel the sun beating down on the back of my neck and the wind tugging at my tee-shirt. Soon Dad would be able to see me.

By the edge of the field was the old chicken run. I knew that I was there because as soon as the birds heard me they ran towards me, squawking and squabbling. Stopping by the coop, I felt the cold metal of the fencing that held them in.

It was then that I heard it. The chickens had suddenly fallen silent. I could hear them running back, scratching as they went, their wings flapping. But they were silent, which was eerie. And then I heard the other sound. Slow, slippery, slithery, something moving through the grass with a gentle hissing sound.

I stood quite still, not daring to breathe. There had never been snakes on Bryher. Everyone said that St Augustine had visited the island and rested here so he had banished all poisonous creatures in repayment for the island's hospitality. But I was sure that it was a snake approaching me. The problem was, I couldn't see where it was. So, I froze like a statue.

Then I felt it slither over my shoe, its thick, dry body running against my ankle. My mouth was quite dry or I might have called to my father. I strained every nerve, listening as hard as I could.

At that moment, I sensed someone else close to me. I heard footsteps and then a thump on the ground as if a stick had been banged down. 'I banished you once before and I banish you again,' said the warm, deep voice of a stranger. The grasses hissed as the snake slithered back towards the shore. And I was alone again . . .

Fiction models

One afternoon my mother asked me to go and fetch my father in from ploughing the old field under Samson Hill.

> Opening sets a task

I made my way down to the shore. Standing there, I listened to the waves rolling on the beach. The sun beat down and I could feel the sand under my feet. I sat down and tugged off my socks. I tied my laces together, slung my shoes over my shoulder and walked along the shore. The sand felt warm and soft under my bare feet. Only the shells dug into my skin.

> Describes what he can hear and feel

Well before Rushy Bay, I stopped. I could hear the distant sound of the old tractor rumbling its way up and down the field. So, I put my shoes back on and made my way towards Samson Hill. I could feel the sun beating down on the back of my neck and the wind tugging at my tee-shirt. Soon Dad would be able to see me.

> The journey made to complete the task

By the edge of the field was the old chicken run. I knew that I was there because as soon as the birds heard me they ran towards me, **squ**awking and **squ**abbling. Stopping by the coop, I felt the cold metal of the fencing that held them in.

> Alliteration creates chicken sounds

It was then that I heard it. The chickens had suddenly fallen silent. I could hear them running back, scratching as they went, their wings flapping. But they were silent, which was eerie. And then I heard the other sound. **S**low, slippery, **s**lithery, **s**omething moving through the grass with a gentle hi**ss**ing sound.

> Dramatic sentence

> Onomatopoeia reflects sound of snake moving

> Dilemma

I stood quite still, not daring to breathe. There had never been snakes on Bryher. Everyone said that St Augustine had visited the island and rested here so he had banished all poisonous creatures in repayment for the island's hospitality. But I was sure that it was a snake approaching me. The problem was, I couldn't see where it was. So, I froze **like a statue.**

> Simile to build picture

> Build-up of tension

Then I felt it slither over my shoe, its thick, dry body running against my ankle. My mouth was quite dry or I might have called to my father. I strained every nerve, listening as hard as I could.

At that moment, I sensed someone else close to me. I heard footsteps and then a thump on the ground as if a stick had been banged down. 'I banished you once before and I banish you again,' said the warm, deep voice of a stranger. The grasses hissed as the snake slithered back towards the shore. And I was alone again . . .

> Useful connective for dramatic moments

> Resolution

29

One afternoon my mother asked me to go and fetch my father in from ploughing the old field under Samson Hill.

I had been cooped up inside all morning so I was relieved to get outside. There was a light mist rolling in from the sea so I pulled on my anorak. I could feel the mist on my face and taste its salty tang. I walked down the shore path till I came to the old boathouse. Pausing, I tilted my head, listening for the sound of my dad's tractor. I could hear it grumbling away like an old man as it struggled up and down the hillside.

I made my way through the hedge and up onto the field. Dad was at the other end. I could hear his tractor turning away from me. He would be followed by the gulls, swooping and diving, searching for any tasty titbits that the plough dug up.

Making my way into the field, I had decided that my best option was to stand in the middle, waving my arms. Surely, that way, he could not miss me. Even though you could hear our tractor from Tresco, I still felt slightly uneasy. Supposing he didn't stop?

I was only a short way into the field when my foot hit something. Something hard and metallic. It had to be something that the plough had dredged up. Probably an old oar or a barrel tie. I stooped down like a crow picking at worms. Whatever it was, it felt cold and hard. Within seconds I realised what it was. A circle of cold metal, with ridges on the edges and what felt like glass set into the outside. It was a circle of metal, a large ring, a crown perhaps.

Without thinking I raised it up high, holding it towards where the sun should have been. All I could hear was the tractor turning at the end of its run, the gulls calling and the distant sea rolling on the shoreline. I stood there, not thinking, just holding the ring of metal, or whatever it was, up to the sky. Then I lowered it down gently onto my head. I could feel the metal sitting heavily, almost biting into the sides of my head.

At that moment two things happened at once. I heard my father calling, 'Bun, over here!' In the same instant, I felt a sudden surge of energy and saw a bright, white light in front of my eyes. I stumbled forwards and cried out loud. You have to remember, I had been blind for so long that to see light was quite a shock . . .

Dobber and the Silver Ring

'What was that?' Amy stared up the lane, peering into the alley. It was very dark and she could see nothing. Not for the first time, she wished that she had a friend to walk home with but since moving school, Amy had not made friends with anyone. She hesitated, then overcame her fear and began to walk up the alley. It was a good shortcut but after school, the boys liked to hang around and leap out on people. It was a silly game and had already got them into trouble with Mr Parker. The alley was dark but it saved at least ten minutes. Her mum liked her home by four.

Halfway along the alley, Amy stopped and stooped down. Carefully, she picked up a small, silver ring, shaped like a fish. It glittered in her hand even though the sun never shone in the alley. Quickening her pace, she tucked it into her pocket and marched on. Just as she came to the end of the alley, there was a noise. She spun round. There was Dobber!

'Give us it,' he demanded, as he walked towards her. Immediately, Amy turned and began to run. At first, she could hear his feet pounding along behind her. As fast as she could, she dashed out of the alley and tore down Smith Street. The world seemed to whirl past. She clenched her fist tight so that she would not drop the ring.

But Dobber was built for bullying and not for speed. Soon, he stopped running. He stood on the corner watching Amy dash like lightning down to the other end of the street where she too stopped. Calmly, she turned to look back at him. Dobber was puffing like an old man.

'Wow,' said someone behind her. Amy turned round. It was Lucy Carter from her class. 'You're really quick.' Amy grinned.

'Not really – it's just that Dobber's not very fast,' Amy said. The girls both laughed. 'He was after this,' continued Amy, holding out the ring, 'I found it in the alley.'

'Oh!' said Lucy, 'that's mine. I lost it ages ago.' Amy handed the ring to Lucy. 'Oh that's so kind of you. You see, my Nan gave it to me and I hadn't dared tell anyone that I'd lost it. You've saved my life!' Lucy smiled as she tucked the ring into her bag.

Amiably, the two girls ambled up Shrubshill Avenue, chatting as they went. Amy knew inside her that she had found two things that day.

Fiction models

Dobber and the Silver Ring

Tag on an '-ing' clause to show what someone is doing

Question opening	**'What was that?'** Amy stared up the lane, **peering into the alley.** It was very dark and she could see nothing. Not for the first time, she wished that she had a friend to walk home with but since moving school, Amy had not made friends with anyone. She hesitated, then overcame her fear and began to walk up the alley. It was a good shortcut but after school, the boys liked to hang around and leap out on people. It was a silly game and had already got them into trouble with Mr Parker. The alley was dark but it saved at least ten minutes. Her mum liked her home by four.

Opening – establishes that main character is lonely

Adverb starter

Description makes ring sound special	Halfway along the alley, Amy stopped and stooped down. **Carefully,** she picked up a **small, silver ring, shaped like a fish.** It glittered in her hand even though the sun never shone in the alley. **Quickening her pace,** she tucked it into her pocket
'-ing' clause as a starter	and marched on. Just as she came to the end of the alley, there was a noise. **She spun round. There was Dobber!**

Main character finds something

Short sentences for drama

Adverb starter

'Give us it,' he demanded, as he walked towards her. **Immediately,** Amy turned and began to run. At first, she could hear his feet **pounding** along behind her. As fast as she could, she **dashed** out of the alley and **tore** down Smith Street. The world seemed to **whirl** past. She **clenched** her fist tight so that she would not drop the ring.

Dilemma – bully tries to take it

Powerful verbs to help action	

But Dobber was built for bullying and not for speed. Soon, he stopped running. He stood on the corner watching Amy dash like lightning down to the other end of the street where she too stopped. **Calmly,** she turned to look back at him. Dobber was puffing **like an old man.**

Escape!

Adverb starter

Simile to build picture	

'Wow,' said someone behind her. Amy turned round. It was Lucy Carter from her class. 'You're really quick.' Amy grinned.

Dialogue kept to a minimum with some action in between so reader can picture what is happening	'Not really – it's just that Dobber's not very fast,' Amy said. The girls both laughed. 'He was after this,' continued Amy, holding out the ring, 'I found it in the alley.'

New friend is found

'Oh!' said Lucy, 'that's mine. I lost it ages ago.' Amy handed the ring to Lucy. 'Oh that's so kind of you. You see, my Nan gave it to me and I hadn't dared tell anyone that I'd lost it. You've saved my life!' Lucy smiled as she tucked the ring into her bag.

Adverb starter to show how the girls feel	**Amiably,** the two girls ambled up Shrubshill Avenue, chatting as they went. Amy knew inside her that she had found two things that day.

Simple ending

33

Tight as a Fist

Brad clenched his fist as tight as a stone and waited. They would be coming down the path any moment now. He tucked himself down behind the bush and held his breath.

Laughing and joking, they passed close by and continued on down the cliff path, towards the beach. He could hear them on the old wooden steps. They creaked as they made their way carefully down. Brad lay back on the grass and stared up at the blue sky. He could still feel the anger swirling around inside of him like some sort of violent wave.

Who wanted to go to the beach anyway? Beaches were for babies and girls who liked to lie in the sun all day and come home looking redder than a radish. From below the cliff, the sound of voices drifted up. They would be swimming now.

Relentlessly, the sun beat down. Nearby, a seedpod popped. The seconds ticked by and Brad began counting. He liked counting. Some days he would count lamp-posts as the school bus trundled into Chester. He counted paving stones, yellow cars and houses with Christmas trees in the windows when it was winter. But now it was summer and they were on holiday. The big family holiday. On a Greek island. Zakynthos. It sounded like a disease.

Brad sat up and stared out, down the cliff. The air was hot and still. The heat seemed to hang on the rocks. Shimmering in the haze like a bright blue ribbon, the distant sea stretched on for ever. The gnarled Cypress trees on the hillside looked like withered limbs. Directly below him, he could see the yellow curve of the bay, the green water giving way to the deeper blue. Black rocks edged the greeny-blue where even now Sonia was sunbathing. Her white body lay stark against the black. Mum wouldn't be pleased. She'd roast alive!

It was at that moment that he saw it. Brad had been about to lever himself up by putting his hand on a small stone. Luckily, he had looked down just in time to see a small brown scorpion. He sat, transfixed, paralysed with fear. His heart thudded.

Brad knew that a sting would hurt. It might mean death. It might mean hospital. He hated hospitals. It made him think about his Gran who had died in one the previous year.

His eyes did not leave the scorpion. He began to wonder if he had been lying on a scorpion. It was a dark chocolate colour, made of tiny segments like a suit of miniature armour. Over its back arched the sting, curved like a scimitar. Its tiny claws were quite still. Carefully, Brad pulled back his hand. The hairs on the back of his neck bristled. His mouth was dry.

Then he heard something rustle in the thin, brown grass. Snakes. It was the first thing that came to him. He sat bolt upright, levered himself up and stepped back onto the path. The grass shivered in the heat. Brad turned and ran onto the cliff path, helter-skeltering down the rickety wooden steps.

His mum sat up and stared as Brad shot off the steps onto the white sand. He looked flustered. She pushed her sunglasses up and smiled. 'I wondered where you'd got to,' she said, lifting a newspaper to shield her eyes.

'There's a scorpion,' he stammered, dashing across the hot sand, feet flying. 'And snakes!' At that moment, the old wooden steps creaked in the heat. It sounded like a gunshot and that was too much for Brad! He dashed past his parents and ran straight into the sea with his arms flailing, sending water flying.

'I don't know,' tutted his mum as she settled back down. 'One minute he's as gloomy as a damp Friday in Margate and the next second he's high as a kite.' Brad's dad shifted his belly, burped and agreed with his wife for the sake of harmony.

In the sea, Brad was already pushing his younger sisters in their inflatable whale up and down. Their laughter bounced against the cliff and echoed back onto the water. Brad couldn't even remember what had annoyed him so much. But he could still see, in his mind, the small, tight dark curve of the scorpion and the grass shivering, shivering.

Fiction models

Humpty

Mrs Dumpty   Now look here, young man. I do not want you hanging around with the free range crowd on the city wall. It's dangerous up there. They're no good that lot and you'll end up in trouble.

Humpty   Oh Mum! It's not fair. Everyone else is allowed down town on a Saturday except me.

Mrs Dumpty   Don't you use that tone of voice with me. I've just about had enough of you today. Now, is that bedroom tidy?

Humpty   *(Sulkily)* Almost.

Mrs Dumpty   Almost! What does almost mean? Either it is or it isn't. Get upstairs and get it tidy. Even Mrs Trotter's piglets keep a clean house – and they're pigs!

Miss Dumpty enters.

Miss Dumpty   Mum, can I go down town to meet Lucy?

Mrs Dumpty   Of course you can dear, but just be careful because that girl is always losing things. Why, only last week she caused such a kerfuffle at the 'Bring and Buy' when she lost her purse.

Miss Dumpty   But Kitty Fisher found it Mum, and Kitty'll be there.

Mrs Dumpty   Well, just you take care. And watch out for that Jack. He's as daft as a brush. Why, only yesterday his mum sent him down to the market with their cow Daisy and he came back without a penny and just three beans.

Miss Dumpty   We don't hang out with him, Mum. See you, Humpty. I'll be back for tea. Bye Mum. *(She exits.)*

Humpty   Why's she allowed to go and I'm not? It's just NOT FAIR!

Fiction models

Humpty

Mrs Dumpty	Now look here, young man. I do not want you hanging around with the free range crowd on the city wall. It's dangerous up there. They're no good that lot and you'll end up in trouble.	Warning opening
Humpty	Oh Mum! It's not fair. Everyone else is allowed down town on a Saturday except me.	
Mrs Dumpty	Don't you use that tone of voice with me. I've just about had enough of you today. Now, is that bedroom tidy?	Make dialogue sound real by using typical things people say
Humpty	*(Sulkily)* Almost.	One-word sentence – typical of speech
Mrs Dumpty	Almost! What does almost mean? Either it is or it isn't. Get upstairs and get it tidy. Even Mrs Trotter's piglets keep a clean house – and they're pigs!	

Notice two techniques for giving stage directions

Miss Dumpty enters.

Miss Dumpty	Mum, can I go down town to meet Lucy?	
Mrs Dumpty	Of course you can dear, but just be careful because that girl is always losing things. Why, only last week she caused such a kerfuffle at the 'Bring and Buy' when she lost her purse.	Notice how mum reacts differently – helps build characters

Reference to nursery rhyme, 'Lucy Locket'

Miss Dumpty	But Kitty Fisher found it Mum, and Kitty'll be there.	
Mrs Dumpty	Well, just you take care. And watch out for that Jack. He's as daft as a brush. Why, only yesterday his mum sent him down to the market with their cow Daisy and he came back without a penny and just three beans.	Use references to other stories for added humour
Miss Dumpty	We don't hang out with him, Mum. See you, Humpty. I'll be back for tea. Bye Mum. *(She exits.)*	
Humpty	Why's she allowed to go and I'm not? It's just NOT FAIR!	Use of capitals for emphasis

Sing a Song

King I'm hungry. What are we having for lunch?

Servant Blackbird Pie, your majesty. Made with the finest blackbirds and baked in a light crust. Served with magic beans.

King And what is for pudding?

Servant Ah, your majesty will not be displeased, I am sure. The Queen of Hearts has made some delicious tarts for your majesty.

King Ah, hah! What sort?

Servant Well, your majesty. We have used only the finest ingredients. Baked in a short-crust pastry, for fifteen minutes by the sandglass, the tarts are a blissful mixture of light custard, cream and strawberries.

King Well, just you make sure that those tarts don't go walking. I was not too pleased last week when I found the platter empty! Heads will roll, I warn you. Well, I'm off to count some money. That always puts me in a better mood.

Servant Yes, your majesty.

The King exits. A maid enters.

Maid OOOh! What's up with his majesty?

Servant He's fed up with people stealing from the kitchen. (*Pause*) It's not you is it?

Maid 'Course not – what'ja take me for? Mark you, I'm not sure about the Knave of Hearts. He's always hanging about . . .

Fiction models

Servant   Enough gossiping. Take the washing out into the garden and hang it up . . . and be quick about it.

Maid   Do I have to? There's a lot of blackbirds in them trees and they don't look too friendly. I reckon it's all on account of the blackbird pie . . .

Fiction models

I think that our playscript was good because we used the story of Humpty Dumpty and that made it easier to write. We had three scenes:

- Humpty asking his mum if he could go out;
- Humpty with the free-range eggs playing 'dare' on the wall;
- Humpty's mum visiting him in the egg hospital.

We managed to make Humpty sound like a teenager by using the sorts of things that teenagers say.

The weakest part of the script was Humpty's sister because she never appeared again.

The best bit about our performance was that some of the lines were quite funny and people did not know how we would end the play.

We could have made it better if everyone had known their lines. In some places the actors were too quiet or said their lines too quickly.

Fiction models

Necessary for leading into reasons	I think that our playscript was good **because** we used the story of Humpty Dumpty and that made it easier to write. We had three scenes:
	What was good
Use of bullet points	• Humpty asking his mum if he could go out; • Humpty with the free-range eggs playing 'dare' on the wall; • Humpty's mum visiting him in the egg hospital.
	We managed to make Humpty sound like a teenager by using the sorts of things that teenagers say.
	What we managed to achieve
	The weakest part of the script was Humpty's sister because she never appeared again.
	Weaknesses
List of simple points – could be improved by adding 'quotes' or more information	The best bit about our performance was that some of the lines were quite funny and people did not know how we would end the play.
	Best part of performance
	We could have made it better if everyone had known their lines. In some places the actors were too quiet or said their lines too quickly.
	Possible improvements

The playscript that our group wrote was successful because we managed to use contrasting characters. For instance, the King sounded very grumpy and the servant used long words. We had a simple structure that focused on the stealing of the tarts by the knave and the maid being wrongfully accused. I think that this kept the audience interested.

The main strength of our performance was that our words were loud and clear and we all used accents so that we could make the characters appear different. The play moved along with a good pace and there were no slow bits.

If I was to criticise the play, I would say that sometimes we stood in front of each other so that the audience could not always see each character. Also, some of us forgot to keep acting when they were not speaking.

The audience seemed to enjoy the play, especially the little ones in Mrs Jenkins' class. They laughed at the funny bits, especially the part with the custard pie.

Fiction models

The Sleeping Sword

When we started reading 'The Sleeping Sword', I thought that the ending was going to be simple because the main character was blind at the beginning. I hoped that by the end of the tale he would be able to see. The writer helped me feel sympathetic towards Bun by showing me what he was thinking and feeling in the first few pages.

I like the way the author gave us a flashback to show how Bun had become blind early on in the story.

The most frightening part of the story was when Bun began to think that he was losing his mind as he kept on forgetting things. The part where he went to the edge of the cliff and was saved by Anna was also frightening.

I did not like the reason that Anna gave for being able to save Bun. She said that she had had a dream and that had woken her in time to see Bun walking towards the cliffs. We are told not use dreams in our stories.

There are no real puzzles in the story. It is a bit strange that the hole appears in the field because Bun's dad has been ploughing that field probably for many years and you would have thought that he would have found it before.

My evaluation so far is that the story is really good because I have got to know the main character and I hope that his blindness disappears.

Michael Morpurgo

The Sleeping Sword

Initial responses

When we started reading 'The Sleeping Sword', **I thought that** the ending was going to be simple because the main character was blind at the beginning. **I hoped that by the end of the tale** he would be able to see. **The writer helped me feel sympathetic towards** Bun by showing me what he was thinking and feeling in the first few pages.

Likes

I like the way the author gave us a flashback to show how Bun had become blind early on in the story.

Most frightening parts

The most frightening part of the story was when Bun began to think that he was losing his mind as he kept on forgetting things. **The part where** he went to the edge of the cliff and was saved by Anna was also frightening.

Dislikes

I did not like the reason that Anna gave for being able to save Bun. She said that she had had a dream and that had woken her in time to see Bun walking towards the cliffs. We are told not use dreams in our stories.

> Useful instructions in bold. Notice how the writer refers to specific incidents to support the points being made

Puzzles

There are no real puzzles in the story. **It is a bit strange that** the hole appears in the field because Bun's dad has been ploughing that field probably for many years and you would have thought that he would have found it before.

Final evaluation

My evaluation so far is that the story is really good because I have got to know the main character and **I hope that** his blindness disappears.

Michael Morpurgo

The Sleeping Sword

We have just started the next part of the story. This section is written in a different typeface and so it suggests that it is like another section of the story. My main prediction is that Bun will use the sword in this part of the story. It may be that he uses it to save someone, probably Anna, and then in some way he gets his eyesight back.

So far this book has been a really good read. The writing is quite easy to read but manages to create a very strong picture in my mind. I like the way that the writer builds up the characters, especially the main character. He reveals Bun's thoughts all the time so that the reader feels as if they are inside his head. This is also because he uses the first person so that it is easier to identify with Bun.

I think too that it is clever the way that Bun goes blind through diving off the quay and then finds the sword by falling into a hole. It is as if the two events are linked. This suggests to me that in some way the sword is going to be important. My other reasons for thinking this is the title of the story, 'The Sleeping Sword', suggests that in some way it will come awake and be used. Another reason for thinking this is that Bun's mum says 'You dive onto rocks instead of into water. You dive down holes that were never there. What next?' This suggests that Bun will do something else adventurous.

My main prediction is that it will be King Arthur's sword because Bun is always reading about him and that Arthur lost it. It could be that he needs the sword to protect the country or to use it in some sort of battle. As a result of finding the sword, I think that Bun will be given his sight back.

My overall evaluation of the story is that the author has managed to develop the main character successfully and I am keen to know what will happen. My only concern is that the end of Michael Morpurgo's books can be sad and so I am wondering if Anna will be all right.

Michael Morpurgo

Axe Soup

Once upon a time there was a traveller who came to a Russian village in the middle of nowhere. He carried a large sack. Inside the sack was a metal cooking pot. He gathered some sticks and made a fire. He put the cooking pot upon the fire and filled it with water from a nearby stream.

The villagers gathered round. They had few visitors in those parts and were curious to see what the traveller was doing.

He took a rusty axe-head from his sack and popped it into the bubbling water. Then he took out a wooden spoon, dipped it into the water and tasted the soup.

'What is it like?' asked a villager.

'It tastes as good as the warm sun,' said the traveller, 'but it needs a few onions and potatoes. Do you have any to spare?' One of the villagers ran inside to fetch a few onions and potatoes. The traveller threw these into the pot and let it boil.

Then he took out his wooden spoon, dipped it into the water and tasted the soup.

'What is it like?' asked a villager.

'It tastes as good as the warm sun,' said the traveller, 'but it needs a few carrots and beans. Do you have any to spare?' One of the villagers ran inside to fetch a few beans. The traveller threw these into the pot and let it boil.

Then he took out a wooden spoon, dipped it into the water and tasted the soup.

 'What is it like?' asked a villager.

'It tastes as good as the warm sun,' said the traveller, 'but it needs a few herbs. Do you have any to spare?' One of the villagers ran inside to fetch some thyme and oregano. The traveller threw the herbs into the pot and let it boil.

Then he took out a wooden spoon, dipped it into the water and tasted the soup.

'Is it ready?' asked a little girl.

'I think it is,' replied the traveller. He served everybody with a bowl full of axe soup. It certainly tasted delicious.

Just before he left the village, he took out the axe and sold it to the villagers for a princely sum. They wanted the traveller's secret ingredient!

And on he travelled, till a few days later he came to another village where he stopped and began to build a fire . . . and inside his sack he had a few stones that he had found on the hillside . . .

Fiction models

Axe Soup

Opening that sets up the trick

Once upon a time there was a **traveller** who came to a Russian **village** in **the middle of nowhere**. He carried a **large sack**. Inside the sack was a **metal cooking pot**. He gathered some sticks and made a fire. He put the cooking pot upon the fire and filled it with water from a nearby stream.

The **villagers** gathered round. They had few visitors in those parts and were curious to see what the traveller was doing.

Pattern that is repeated four times

1 He took a **rusty axe-head** from his sack and popped it into the bubbling water. Then he took out a **wooden spoon**, dipped it into the water and tasted the **soup**.

'What is it like?' asked a villager.

'It tastes **as good as the warm sun**,' said the traveller, 'but it needs a few **onions** and **potatoes**. Do you have any to spare?' One of the villagers ran inside to fetch a few onions and potatoes. The traveller threw these into the pot and let it boil.

2 Then he took out his wooden spoon, dipped it into the water and tasted the soup.

'What is it like?' asked a villager.

'It tastes as good as the warm sun,' said the traveller, 'but it needs a few **carrots** and **beans**. Do you have any to spare?' One of the villagers ran inside to fetch a few beans. The traveller threw these into the pot and let it boil.

3 Then he took out a wooden spoon, dipped it into the water and tasted the soup.

'What is it like?' asked a villager.

'It tastes as good as the warm sun,' said the traveller, 'but it needs a **few herbs**. Do you have any to spare?' One of the villagers ran inside to fetch some **thyme** and **oregano**. The traveller threw the herbs into the pot and let it boil.

Elements that could be changed are in bold

4 Then he took out a wooden spoon, dipped it into the water and tasted the soup.

'Is it ready?' asked a little girl.

'I think it is,' replied the traveller. He served everybody with a bowl full of **axe soup**. It certainly tasted delicious.

The trick!

Just before he left the village, he took out the axe and sold it to the villagers for a princely sum. They wanted the traveller's secret ingredient!

The story begins again!

And on he travelled, till a few days later he came to **another village** where he stopped and began to build a fire ... and inside his sack he had a **few stones** that he had found on the hillside ...

Three Golden Peaches

When did you last smell a peach? It is not surprising that something so soft and sweet, so juicy and fragrant is considered to be magical. In Italy, they believe that burying peach leaves will cure a wart. In Texas, the leaves have to be boiled in water and made into peach tea to ward off a bad stomach ache.

But the peach is most loved in China. There the peach is considered to bring long life and its blossom can keep evil spirits out of a house. Children wear necklaces with a peach stone on them for protection. It is believed that if a soul ate a peach from the tree of life, it would give 3,000 years of good health.

Now, once there was a King and Queen whose daughter fell ill. She was so ill that all the doctors and physicians could find no cure. Why, they didn't even know what was wrong with her! Day by day she grew paler and paler. Day by day she grew stiller and stiller. Her mother sat with her and her father paced up and down.

One day a red-faced farmer came to the city and boasted that he knew how to cure the girl. Sooner rather than later, he was dragged before the King who demanded to know what he meant. The farmer told him that he had heard tell of a magical peach tree that grew in a garden where night-ingales sang, hidden in the furthermost corner of the kingdom. It was said that even a bite of one of these peaches would cure any disease.

So it was that the King ordered his guards to travel throughout the king-dom, to find the tree of life. Meanwhile, the farmer left the city sitting on a donkey whose saddlebags were full of gold.

But one by one the soldiers returned, having found nothing. By now the King was at the end of his tether. The Queen sat patiently watching her daughter grow paler and thinner. Why, she was paler than the lilies that grew by the river.

But one day, into the furthermost corner of the kingdom the message drift-ed, carried on the breeze, into a garden where the nightingales sang and a peach tree grew. There lived not one, not two, but three brothers. The oldest said, 'I am the oldest and therefore I shall take the princess a peach.' He went to the end of the garden and plucked a peach. He put it in a basket, covered it with a cloth so that it would neither spoil nor ruin, and off he set.

He climbed the great mountain. He forded the great river. He walked through the great forest. On the third day he met a frail old lady who said, 'I'm starving. Have you got a bite for a poor old lady?' But the boy hid the basket and said, 'No, leave me be, old woman.' But she pointed to the basket and asked what he was hiding. He stammered, 'Only worms for fishing.'

'Then worms let it be,' she muttered.

Later that day, the boy reached the city and was taken before the King. He placed the basket on the King's lap and said that he had brought a peach for the girl. The King felt under the cloth. At that moment a snake slid out of the basket, followed by another and then another. Hissing, they slithered onto the floor, their forked tongues flickering.

'A trick,' yelled the King, and the boy was booted out of the city. When he reached home, the second brother took the basket and went to the end of the garden. There he plucked a peach, put it in a basket, covered it with a cloth so that it would neither spoil nor ruin, and set off.

He too climbed the great mountain. He forded the great river. He walked through the great forest. On the third day he met a frail old lady who said, 'I'm starving. Have you got a bite for a poor old lady?' But the boy hid the basket and said, 'No, leave me be, old woman.' But she pointed to the basket and asked what he was hiding. He stammered, 'Only frogs' legs for tea.'

'Then frogs let it be,' she muttered.

Later that day, the boy reached the city and was taken before the King. He placed the basket on the King's lap and said that he had brought a peach for the girl. The King felt under the cloth and at that moment a frog leaped out of the basket, followed by another and then another.

'A trick,' yelled the King and the boy was booted out of the city. When he reached home, the third brother took the basket, and even though the others scoffed at him, he went to the end of the garden, where he plucked not one, not two but three ripe peaches. He put them in a basket, covered them with a cloth so that they would neither spoil nor ruin, and set off.

He too climbed the great mountain where he watched the eagles wheel in the sky as the sun set. He forded the great river where he watched the brown bear scoop salmon from the icy mountain waters. He walked through the great forest where the sunlight dared not creep. On the third day, he met a frail old lady who said, 'I'm starving. Have you got a bite for a poor old lady?' So the boy gave her one of the peaches. She took a bite and as she ate he could see her skin begin to glow, her hair shine and she straightened her crooked back.

'God speed,' she muttered.

Later that day, the boy reached the city and was taken before the King. He placed the basket on the King's lap and said that he had brought a peach for the girl. The King felt under the cloth and brought out the two peaches. How sweet they smelled. The King seized the basket and ran down the corridor towards the room where the princess lay. The boy chased after him.

They burst into the room. But the Queen held up her hand. She turned to her husband who stood there holding the peaches and she shook her head.

'Too late,' she murmured. They all turned to look at the princess, cold and still as a marble statue. The boy took a feather from her pillow and held it under her nose. But the feather did not move. So he took a mirror from the wall and held it to her face – and yes, it misted. She was still alive!

So, he took a peach and held it to her lips, pleading her to take but one bite. And as she did, the tiniest of nibbles and peach juice dribbled down her lips. And as the juice slipped between her lips, colour began to flush her cheeks. Then she took another tiny bite and she opened her eyes. Then she took another bite and with that she sat up in bed. Grabbing the peach, she began to eat as if she had not eaten for days. She finished the peach and hurled the stone out of the window. Then she ate the second one and by then she was as young and healthy as she had ever been.

Now of course, you know without me telling you that the boy married the princess . . . but what you do not know is that those two peach stones that she had thrown out of the window grew into peach trees overnight. All summer they blossomed and the peaches were gold, silver and copper. Now, the King put a fence around the trees for it was obvious that they too were magical and who knows what might happen . . . if some unsuspecting person should come by and eat one . . .

The Ants and the Grasshopper

It was autumn time. The leaves were frosty and the ground was hard as an axe blade.

The ants were busy moving grains of wheat from their store into the anthill.

A grasshopper happened to hop by. It was cold and almost starving for it had not had a nibble in weeks. It stopped and asked the ants if they would share a morsel.

'What were you doing this summer?' asked the ants who had been busy all summer long, storing food for winter.

'Why, I was busy singing all day and night,' replied the grasshopper.

'Well then,' said the ants, 'as you kept yourself so busy all summer with singing, you can keep yourself busy all winter by dancing.'

Then they shut their food store and disappeared into their nest.

Fiction models

TERM 2: **FABLES**
(Easier)

The Ants and the Grasshopper

Opening sets the scene

It was autumn time. The leaves were **frosty** and the ground was **hard as an axe blade**.

Description to show how hostile the place is

The workers

The ants were busy moving grains of wheat from their store into the anthill.

The lazy one

A grasshopper happened to hop by. It was cold and almost starving for it had not had a nibble in weeks. It stopped and asked the ants if they would share a morsel.

Explains how lazy one idled

'What were you doing this summer?' asked the ants who had been busy all summer long, storing food for winter.

'Why, I was busy singing all day and night,' replied the grasshopper.

Brief dialogue

Response

'Well then,' said the ants, 'as you kept yourself so busy all summer with singing, you can keep yourself busy all winter by dancing.'

Ending

Then they shut their food store and disappeared into their nest.

Blunt ending

The Blacksmith and his Dog

Once upon a time there was a blacksmith who had a dog.

All day long the blacksmith sweated at the forge.

He chopped the wood to feed the fire.
He puffed the bellows to make it roar.
He beat the metal to bring the shape.
He bent the bar to shoe the horse.

And of course, he cooled the iron to fix the shape in the great water butt outside. It hissed like a snake, sending steam into the air.

All the while, the dog slept in the corner.

But when the blacksmith sat down for his dinner, the dog woke up.

'Lazybones!' shouted the blacksmith, 'you sleep while there is work to be done and you only wake when there is food to be eaten.

Moral of these tales: Lazybones, who prefer sleep or play to hard work, run the risk of hunger.

How Night Came

*Now before there was night,
There was only light –
And this is the story
Of how darkness came.*

During the day, the sun shone and in the evening along came the moon so bright that it was light all the time.

God called the bat and gave him a basket tied up tight. Bat was told to fly to the moon with the basket. So bat set out, but the journey was long and the journey was hard. In the end poor bat became so tired, he had to stop to rest.

While bat slept, some other creatures came along. Curious about the contents of the basket, they approached. Some say it was coyote but I don't know the truth ... anyway, one of them opened the basket just in case there was something good to eat inside.

Too late – out leapt the darkness.

You can imagine the animals' surprise. One moment it was quite bright and the next moment it was pitch dark. They all stared up at the moon, grateful for its thin, silvery light.

Ever since then, poor old bat has had to sleep all day because at night he is too busy frantically fluttering about, still trying to catch the darkness to take it to the moon.

From Sierra Leone

Fiction models

How Night Came

Chant used to introduce story	*Now before there was night,* *There was only light –* *And this is the story* *Of how darkness came.*
Context set	**During the day,** the sun shone and in the evening along came the moon so bright that it was light all the time.
Task given to creature	God called the bat and gave him a basket tied up tight. Bat was told to fly to the moon with the basket. **So** bat set out, but the journey was long and the journey was hard. **In the end** poor bat became so tired, he had to stop to rest.
Others interfere	**While** bat slept, some other creatures came along. Curious about the contents of the basket, they approached. Some say it was coyote but I don't know the truth … anyway, one of them opened the basket just in case there was something good to eat inside.
Dilemma!	**Too late** – out leapt the darkness.
Result	You can imagine the animals' surprise. **One moment** it was quite bright and the next moment it was pitch dark. They all stared up at the moon, grateful for its thin, silvery light.
End	**Ever since** then, poor old bat has had to sleep all day because at night he is too busy frantically fluttering about, still trying to catch the darkness to take it to the moon.

From Sierra Leone

Useful connectives (in bold) for organising events

Why the Robin has a Red Chest

Years ago, at the dawn of time, there was only one fire and the task of making sure that it was kept alight fell to an old man and a young lad. The old man would sit up all day long and tend to the fire. At night, it was the boy's turn.

All night long the lad sat there, stoking the fire, adding on more branches if it ever looked as if it might go out.

Now, as you can imagine, it was hard to keep awake. One night he fell asleep. Gradually, the fire began to burn down. Soon there were only a few glowing embers left.

All this time a wolf had been watching. Now wolves do not like fire. In fact they hate it. So the wolf was pleased to see the only fire on earth dying out. It sat in the forest watching the boy nodding off and the fire gradually dying down. Just as it seemed to have finally faded and the boy was fast asleep, the wolf crept out of the forest. Padding silently over to the fire, it stood staring at the last embers. Its eyes glowed red in the reflection.

The wolf decided to finish the job. It turned its back on the fire and, with a few quick kicks, scuffed up enough dirt to smother the dying embers. Then it trotted back into the forest.

Now that could easily have been the end of fire for a long while. However, a robin had been perched on a branch of a fir tree, watching what was happening. As soon as the wolf had disappeared, the robin flew down to the fire. Hovering above the tiniest of sparks, it began to flap its wings, frantically fanning the flames. Slowly, the ember began to glow until in the end the fire burst into light again.

Sadly, in saving the fire, the robin branded its chest with a red streak of flame, which it still carries to this day.

From Ireland

The Legend of Randwick

Well, I guess you've heard the big old legends about the likes of Robin Hood and King Arthur. Now this is a local legend because it is all about a village just a stone's throw over the hill from where I live . . . and that village is called Randwick.

Now all this took place a long time ago – old Heggerty was cooking up a stew when she got called down the lane to mind a lamb that was being born. Now she'd not got far with that stew. In fact she'd only just put on the water and added in one onion so it wasn't much of a stew at all!

Well, her two boys came back from the farm where they'd been mending fences. They were called Tom and Dick and they were big lads. They didn't want to wait for their Ma to come back so they set about adding to that stew.

First, they added in some potatoes that they found in an old sack. Next they added in some carrots and a turnip. In fact they kept on adding in bits of this and bits of that. They found a nice piece of crackling left over from the pig and a couple of trotters. Then they found the pig's head! Yes, they even added that to the stew.

Just then they heard their Ma coming back so they slammed on the lid and sat down.

'That smells good,' said their Ma, as she came into the kitchen. Tom and Dick just sat at the table grinning.

Old Ma Heggerty took off the stew lid to take a good sniff of her stew. As she lifted the lid, up bobbed the pig's head with its eyes goggling right up at her and its snout just open as if it was about to speak! Well, that was too much of a fright for her. You should have heard her scream.

She grabbed Tom's hand and ran out of the kitchen shouting, 'Run Dick, run Dick,' as loud as she could. She ran down the hill yelling and screaming at her son, 'Run Dick,' as if the devil himself were chasing her. And everyone who lived there stopped what they were doing and came out to look at old Ma Heggerty and her two boys running away from that pig's head stew.

Now even to this day, the village is named after that event which everyone heard about in the five valleys around Stroud. Run Dick – Randwick . . .

Snip snap snout
My story's out.

The Legend of Randwick

Note use of informal language (in bold)

Preamble

Well, I guess you've heard the big old legends about the likes of Robin Hood and King Arthur. **Now this is** a local legend because it is all about a village **just a stone's throw** over the hill from where I live . . . and that village is called Randwick.

Opening

Now all this took place a long time ago – old Heggerty was cooking up a stew when she got called down the lane to mind a lamb that was being born. Now she'd not got far with that stew. In fact she'd only just put on the water and added in one onion so it wasn't much of a stew at all!

Build-up of events

Well, her two boys came back from the farm where they'd been mending fences. They were called Tom and Dick and they were big lads. They didn't want to wait for their Ma to come back so they set about adding to that stew.

First, they added in some potatoes that they found in an old sack. Next they added in some carrots and a turnip. In fact they kept on adding in bits of this and bits of that. They found a nice piece of crackling left over from the pig and a couple of trotters. Then they found the pig's head! Yes, they even added that to the stew.

Dilemma

Just then they heard their Ma coming back so they slammed on the lid and sat down.

'That smells good,' said their Ma, as she came into the kitchen. Tom and Dick just sat at the table grinning.

Events that follow on

Old Ma Heggerty took off the stew lid to take a good sniff of her stew. As she lifted the lid, up bobbed the pig's head with its eyes goggling right up at her and its snout just open as if it was about to speak! Well, that was too much of a fright for her. You should have heard her scream.

Resolution

She grabbed Tom's hand and ran out of the kitchen shouting, 'Run Dick, run Dick,' as loud as she could. She ran down the hill yelling and screaming at her son, 'Run Dick,' as if the devil himself were chasing her. And everyone who lived there stopped what they were doing and came out to look at old Ma Heggerty and her two boys running away from that pig's head stew.

Ending

Now even to this day, the village is named after that event which everyone heard about in the five valleys around Stroud. Run Dick – Randwick . . .

Rhyming couplet – traditional end

Snip snap snout
My story's out.

The Children of Hamelin

If you had been in the little town of Hamelin, in Germany, in the year 1284 you would not have liked it. I know, because rats are not liked by most people and this town had a plague of them. There were rats everywhere – in the gutters, in the cupboards, under the tables, on the beams – it seemed as if they would never be rid of them! Even the town cats had packed up shop and left!

Well, that year a stranger arrived in town. You couldn't miss him – he wore a long flowing coat made of many bright colours. Many joked that it was Joseph – and soon he became known as Brightman. Word got around that he had said that he could rid the town of their problem – for the right sum of money. The elders of the town met and agreed that if indeed he could rid the town of rats, they would pay him handsomely.

Well, the deal was sealed with a shake of the hand and no sooner than this was agreed Brightman pulled out a strange pipe and began to play a melodious tune. The townsfolk were amazed because all the rats began to stream out of the houses and barns, following Brightman as he strode through the streets. What a sight it was. The tall piper leading the way, followed by a thousand rats squealing and squeaking after him. It looked like a living river streaming out behind him.

Brightman led his strange procession out of the town, across the down and on to where the Weser River flowed. There he paused, before taking off his coat and plunging into the waters. Amazingly, the rats followed, thousands of them swarming into the water till for a moment it seemed to boil with their bodies. But the current there is strong and a few moments later there was silence. The rats had drowned and already their bodies were drifting down the stream to wash up on the banks over the next few miles where they lay rotting for the next few weeks.

Now, Brightman put on his coat and strode back into the town where he was welcomed as a hero. Everyone stood clapping him on the back and cheering. But as the days went by, the town elders began to regret that they had promised so much money. They began to make excuses and some even pretended, and maybe had begun to believe, that the plague had not been that much of a problem anyway. In the end they refused to pay Brightman the money that was due.

It was a few days later that Brightman returned on a feast day when the people of the town were in the streets celebrating. This time he wore a cloak as red as blood and wore a strange mask. Once again he began to play, only this time it was not the rats that followed but the children. Every child in Hamelin followed the piper as if mesmerised by the melody that he played. The adults suspected no ill, for it seemed to them like a party game.

But the piper led them out of the town, across the down and into the mountains. And not one child was ever seen again.

Fiction models

Nail Stew

Once upon a time there was a salesman who came to a small town by a river. He carried a large suitcase. Inside the case was an old iron wok. He gathered some sticks and made a fire. He put the pan upon the fire and filled it with water from the river.

Soon some of the town's people gathered round. They were curious to see what the salesman was doing.

He took a shiny nail from his case and dropped it into the bubbling water. Then he took out a spoon, dipped it into the water and tasted the stew.

'What is it like?' asked somebody.

'It tastes as good as sweet sugarcane,' said the salesman, 'but it needs some spices. Do you have any to spare?' One person ran off to fetch some spices. So, the salesman threw these into the wok and let it boil.

Then he took out his spoon, dipped it into the water and tasted the stew.

'What is it like?' asked somebody.

'It tastes as good as sweet sugarcane,' said the salesman, 'but it needs some chunks of meat. Do you have any to spare?' One person ran inside to fetch some meat. So, the salesman threw the meat into the wok and let it boil.

Then he took out a spoon, dipped it into the water and tasted the stew.

'What is it like?' asked somebody.

'It tastes as good as sweet sugarcane,' said the salesman, 'but it needs some vegetables. Do you have any to spare?' One person ran inside to fetch some potatoes, a carrot and an onion. So, the salesman dropped these into the wok and let it boil.

'What is it like?' asked somebody.

'It tastes as good as sweet sugarcane,' said the salesman, 'but it needs a lashing of tabasco sauce to give it a tang. Do you have any to spare?' One person ran inside to fetch some tabasco sauce. So, the salesman dribbled some drops of tabasco sauce into the wok and let it boil.

Then he took out a spoon, dipped it into the water and tasted the stew.

'Is it ready?' asked a little boy.

'Indeed, I think it is,' replied the salesman. He served everybody with a bowl full of nail stew. It certainly tasted delicious.

Just before he left the town, he took out the shiny nail and sold it to one of the people who owned a café. They wanted the salesman's secret ingredient!

And on he travelled, till a few days later he came to another town where he stopped and began to build a fire . . . and inside his case he had a few more shiny nails . . .

The Car Salesman and His Apprentice

Once upon a time there was a car salesman who was to take on a young lad. It might have been from the local secondary school for work experience or perhaps it was the new government Youth Work Place Scheme. I'm not sure.

The salesman was at work first thing in the morning and stayed till late at night. All day long he worked as hard as he could to sell cars.

He polished the cars till they shone like gold.
He swept the forecourt so there were no leaves.
He spoke on the phone till his voice was hoarse.
He filed the papers to keep them tidy.

And of course, he spent time with the customers, making sure that he fixed the sale at just the right price. A profit for him and a bargain for them. That way, so he said, everyone wins. And who could disagree with such a statement?

All day the young lad hung around or sat in the waiting room, reading car magazines and drinking capuccino from the vending machine. Whenever there was something to do, he could not be found.

But at the end of the day, things were different. It was the salesman's habit to count up the day's takings before locking up the shop. As he made ready to leave, the young lad leapt to life, offered to lock up the cars and close the doors. He was fussing around, busying himself with locks and keys.

'Idle youth!' shouted the salesman, 'You doss around when the shop is busy with customers! You disappear when there is work to be done!

Fiction models

You seem unable to see work when it is obvious that tidying, sweeping or polishing needs to be done! In fact, you only come to life when the work is done and the money is to be handed out! Don't bother coming back tomorrow!'

Moral of this story: Lazybones will earn only an empty hand and hours of time.

The Stormy Rescue

It must have been about two o'clock that night when Aunt Millie awoke. The rain had slackened but it was still dark outside.

She had left the window down just in case the fox came back. That was what pulled her up out of her sleep – two short, sharp barks.

Aunt Millie gave Uncle Fred a shove to wake him. She tugged on her thin cotton robe and made her way downstairs.

She flicked on the porch light and squinted out through the side windows.

To her amazement, there was Tom. As she said later, he looked just like a drowned turkey standing there on the porch, dripping with rain and his face turned down at the edges.

She tut-tutted and flung the door open at once, drawing Tom in.

He was soaking wet. So she went off down to the kitchen range to fetch a warm towel.

What was that boy thinking about? Why, hadn't she known all along that given half the chance he would be out of that bedroom window onto the tree. Boys – they just couldn't resist something like that.

Fiction models

The Stormy Rescue

Main character awakes

It must have been about two o'clock that night when Aunt Millie awoke. The rain had **slackened** but it was still dark outside.

Powerful verb adds to atmosphere

What woke her?

She had left the window down just in case the fox came back. That was what pulled her up out of her sleep – two **sh**ort, **sh**arp barks.

Why?

Alliteration makes line more powerful

Goes down stairs

Aunt Millie gave Uncle Fred a shove to wake him. She tugged on her **thin** cotton robe and made her way downstairs.

What does the word 'thin' suggest?

She flicked on the porch light and **squinted** out through the side windows.

Why does she need to squint?

Finds Tom

To her amazement, there was Tom. As she said later, he looked just like a drowned turkey standing there on the porch, dripping with rain and his face turned down at the edges.

Longer sentence to build description

She tut-tutted and flung the door open at once, drawing Tom in.

Notice use of simple, short paragraphs

Her reactions

He was soaking wet. So she went off down to the kitchen range to fetch a warm towel.

What she is thinking

What was that boy thinking about? Why, hadn't she known all along that given half the chance he would be out of that bedroom window onto the tree. Boys – they just couldn't resist something like that.

Questions also prompt the reader to think

The Stormy Rescue

It must have been about two o'clock that night when Uncle Fred awoke. The rain had slackened but it was still dark outside.

He could hear Aunt Millie shuffling around, pulling on her robe and making her way downstairs. It was probably that darned fox, he thought, as he grabbed his old coat and made after her.

But as he came down the stairs, he could see that someone was standing on the porch, drenched and bedraggled.

'Who is it?' Uncle Fred asked, tugging his pants over his pyjamas. He stopped and stared. It was Tom, muttering something about letting the baby fox out.

Uncle Fred, not one to leap to conclusions, paused and stared at the boy, looking right into his eyes. And there he saw the truth. A mixture of worry and guilt that he recognised.

Yes, now it all slotted into place. Tom had let the baby fox go because he could not bear to see a wild creature caged, or killed for that matter.

Fred swallowed. He knew that feeling. He'd once hand-reared a baby fox as a lad and still remembered the day that it had been caught in one of his father's traps. Well, perhaps Tom was right. At least after tonight, the fox would not be coming back.

Foxes were clever like that.

Fiction models

'Don't you go mucking around with that Petie Burkis,' snapped mum. 'Your Aunt Millie is calling round for tea on her way back home and I want you here. All right?' Trying to look innocent, I nodded my head, grabbed my school bag and was off.

But we always walked home together after school, inventing newspaper headlines for the day's events. One day Petie was going to be a newspaper editor. I pretended that I was going to be an ace reporter but actually I wanted to be a vet. I had found the airplane timetable for Kenya in a travel agents and knew exactly which flight I would take when I had my first job. I was going to work on a game reserve, pulling thorns out of elephants' feet and treating lion cubs. I had it all worked out.

Well, that afternoon we were almost home. In fact we were coming down the alley behind Petie's house. It must have been garbage day because everyone had their bins out. And there it was. Sitting right on top of this lady's garbage like a present waiting for two boys to come along and claim it.

It was an old mayonnaise jar. But not just any old jar. It was crammed full of marbles. We grabbed it and ran up the alley till we came to Petie's place. We stretched out in his back yard and unscrewed the lid. Out tumbled hundreds of marbles. Some we had never seen before. They were giant gobstopper marbles, tigers' eyes, and colour bombs.

We divided the pile up and began to play. Petie's yard is just right because the concrete is smooth but there are some good lines that can be used to roll a marble along and be certain of hitting any lying around on the line.

I got so engrossed in what we were doing that I forgot all about the time. Suddenly, I remembered. Aunt Millie! 'Oh no!' I exclaimed, grabbing my bag and running for it. Petie gathered up my marbles and as I ran I knew that he would claim that I had

Fiction models

left him mid-game so that he was entitled to any marbles left in play. But it was too late to worry about that.

A few minutes later, I arrived home. Puffing and panting, I dashed into the kitchen. Angrily, my mother stood there glaring at me. She fixed me with a terrible stare. Aunt Millie was nowhere to be seen. 'You haven't been round at Petie's house have you?' asked my mother. I shook my head . . . just as Petie's mother came into the kitchen.

I groaned. They'd caught me out and I knew that I was looking at being grounded – at the least . . . So, I had a punishment on its way for missing Aunt Millie, another for lying, and not only that. I had also lost all the marbles to Petie. I lay on my bed and stared at the cracks in the ceiling.

I imagined what the papers would say: 'Boy Suffers Triple Hardship', 'Major Blow to Marbles' Champ', or maybe 'Boy Loses His Marbles'. Yes, that was just right. 'Boy Loses His Marbles'.

Fiction models

TERM 3: **NEW CHAPTER IN STYLE OF AUTHOR**
(Easier)

| Warning opening | 'Don't you go mucking around with that Petie Burkis,' **snapped** mum. 'Your Aunt Millie is calling round for tea on her way back home and I want you here. All right?' **Trying to look innocent,** I nodded my head, grabbed my school bag and was off. | Verb suggests she means it! / '-ing' clause to show how he is acting |

But we always walked home together after school, inventing newspaper headlines for the day's events. One day Petie was going to be a newspaper editor. I pretended that I was going to be an ace reporter but actually I wanted to be a vet. I had found the airplane timetable for Kenya in a travel agents and knew exactly which flight I would take when I had my first job. I was going to work on a game reserve, pulling thorns out of elephants' feet and treating lion cubs. I had it all worked out.

Build-up — Reveals that he is a dreamy character

Well, that afternoon we were almost home. In fact we were coming down the alley behind Petie's house. It must have been **garbage day** because everyone had their bins out. And there it was. Sitting right on top of this lady's garbage like a present waiting for two boys to come along and claim it.

Temptation! — 'garbage day' shows story is set in another place

It was an old mayonnaise jar. But not just any old jar. It was **crammed** full of marbles. We **grabbed** it and ran up the alley till we came to Petie's place. We **stretched** out in his back yard and unscrewed the lid. Out **tumbled** hundreds of marbles. Some we had never seen before. They were giant gobstopper marbles, tigers' eyes, and colour bombs.

Dilemma – the warning is forgotten — Use of fairly short sentences and well-chosen verbs

We divided the pile up and began to play. Petie's **yard** is just right because the concrete is smooth but there are some good lines that can be used to roll a marble along and be certain of hitting any lying around on the line.

Dilemma, continued — Another American term

I got so engrossed in what we were doing that I forgot all about the time. **Suddenly, I remembered.** Aunt Millie! 'Oh no!' I exclaimed, **grabbing** my bag and running for it. Petie gathered up my marbles and as I ran I knew that he would claim that I had

Main character realises that warning has been broken — Useful way to reintroduce warning / Add an action

71

Fiction models

left him mid-game so that he was entitled to any marbles left in play. But it was too late to worry about that.

Adverb starter

Arrives home – and lies!

A few minutes later, I arrived home. **Puffing and panting,** I dashed into the kitchen. **Angrily,** my mother stood there glaring at me. She fixed me with a terrible stare. Aunt Millie was nowhere to be seen. 'You haven't been round at Petie's house have you?' asked my mother. I shook my head . . . just as Petie's mother came into the kitchen.

'-ing' clause to start sentence to emphasise how hard he has run

Caught out and punished

I groaned. They'd caught me out and I knew that I was looking at being grounded – at the least . . . So, I had a punishment on its way for missing Aunt Millie, another for lying, and not only that. I had also lost all the marbles to Petie. I lay on my bed and **stared at the cracks in the ceiling**.

Short sentence for impact

Use of detail makes narrative sound real

End

I imagined what the papers would say: 'Boy Suffers Triple Hardship', 'Major Blow to Marbles' Champ', or maybe 'Boy Loses His Marbles'. Yes, that was just right. 'Boy Loses His Marbles'.

In the novel, Petie invents news headlines for daily events

'Don't go down by the old creek,' said Aunt Millie, as she rolled the dough out on the kitchen table. Tom shook his head as he watched the dough stretch out like rubber.

Half an hour later, he was down by the hill. The trees so were so big that they looked like giants striding along. Tom stood underneath one and stared up the trunk into the branches. It was like being inside a church and looking up one of the stone pillars. He tried putting his arms round one but could not. Grinning, he imagined the headline 'Boy Hugs Tree'.

Tom left the trees and made his way across the butterfly meadow. They swarmed up out of the grasses in thousands. It looked like a mass of shimmering flowers rising up into the air and then settling back again. He passed the place where he had first seen the black fox leaping over the crest of the hill in the long, green grass. Tom paused and stared expectantly – but the fox was not there. So, he trudged on in the summery heat and made his way down to the creek.

Water swirled round the bend in the river, thick and muddy. Midges danced on the surface. The heat shimmered. It was so hot that it seemed like a good idea. Tugging off his socks and sandals, he began to wade in. The water felt so cool. At first, it was like a shock and he had to stand still while his hot skin adjusted. Soon he was wading in deeper. He stopped to roll up his shorts and at that moment stepped forwards, onto a sharp object. He cried out in pain and, at the same time, he stumbled.

It was dark under the water and then Tom found himself bursting through the surface and spluttering. It was also deep for he could no longer touch the bottom and the current was tugging him further out. Desperately, he began to strike out for the bank but although he did not go under again, he made little headway. His tee-shirt and shorts seemed to drag him back. His arms ached so he let himself drift, out into the mainstream and away round the bend.

Tom drifted on for a while, heart thudding, mind racing. He could go on for ever like this. Perhaps he'd end up at the sea? But as he rounded another bend, he saw a tree that had fallen into the river and had caught fast. It was jutting out. He swam as hard as he could towards it and managed to grab one of the wet, black branches. Although they were slippery and covered in slime, he still clung on.

A short while later, Tom was on the bank. He stood for a while just dripping and enjoying the sensation of being alive, on the bank and safe again. Then he began his journey back to the farm. His clothes steamed in the hot, sunny afternoon. He smelled of the river. Irritatingly, a swarm of flies trailed him.

He just hoped that Aunt Millie didn't catch him. There'd be no supper if she did. After all, she had warned him!

Non-fiction models

Extracts from the Ugly Sister's Letters to her Cousin, Gertie

Dear Gertie   *Tuesday evening*

This morning a palace footman arrived with an invitation to the Prince's Ball. We all know that he is looking for a wife, so there was great excitement.

Before lunch, Esmerelda and I went shopping for new ball-gowns. We have to look our smartest. I chose a beautiful gown that is bright yellow and lime green with purple spots. Esmerelda made a terrible mistake by choosing a gown that is scarlet and covered in pink splodges. She looked like a large, pink donut with tomato sauce on top. But I didn't tell her. Well, I don't want any competition at the Ball.

In the afternoon, Cinderella had the cheek to ask if she could go to the Ball too. Well, we soon put her right on that account. She has far too much work in the kitchen. Anyway, I noticed some mice down there and they need catching.

Dear Gertie   *Saturday evening*

This evening my sister and I went to the Prince's Ball with our new father, Baron Hardup. Mother only married him for his money. He is SO STUPID. He kept on worrying about leaving Cinderella cleaning the kitchen.

First, we danced with every young man available. But there was a disaster as the prince only danced with one beautiful girl.

At midnight there was a great drama as the girl ran away. It was very strange. The clock struck twelve and off she went as if her knickers were on fire. I saw the coach shoot by. The footmen looked very whiskery. Not at all nice.

Next, someone noticed that the prince's girl had left behind a glass slipper. The prince said that he would find and marry the girl whose foot fits the slipper. I can't wait for him to visit our house. I'm sure my foot will fit and if it doesn't, I'll squeeze it in somehow!

Extracts from the Ugly Sister's Letters to her Cousin, Gertie

Dear Gertie   *Tuesday evening*

This morning a palace footman arrived with an invitation to the Prince's Ball. We all know that he is looking for a wife, so there was **great** excitement.

Before lunch, Esmerelda and I went shopping for new ball-gowns. We have to look our smartest. I chose a beautiful gown that is bright yellow and lime green with purple spots. Esmerelda made a terrible mistake by choosing a gown that is scarlet and covered in pink splodges. **She looked like a large, pink donut with tomato sauce on top. But I didn't tell her. Well, I don't want any competition at the Ball.**

In the afternoon, Cinderella had the cheek to ask if she could go to the Ball too. Well, we soon put her right on that account. She has far too much work in the kitchen. Anyway, I noticed **some mice** down there and they need catching.

Dear Gertie   *Saturday evening*

This evening my sister and I went to the Prince's Ball with our new father, Baron Hardup. Mother only married him for his money. He is SO STUPID. He kept on worrying about leaving Cinderella cleaning the kitchen.

First, we danced with every young man available. But there was a disaster as the prince only danced with one beautiful girl.

At midnight there was a great drama as the girl ran away. It was very strange. The clock struck twelve and off she went as if her knickers were on fire. I saw the coach shoot by. The footmen looked very **whiskery**. Not at all nice.

Next, someone noticed that the prince's girl had left behind a glass slipper. The prince said that he would find and marry the girl whose foot fits the slipper. I can't wait for him to visit our house. I'm sure my foot will fit and if it doesn't, I'll squeeze it in somehow!

Note use of temporal correctives to organise the sequence of events

Add in views and comments

Use names

Show character through comments made

Reference to mice who will become coachmen

Reference back to the mice

The Green Van

He was called Mr Savage. He did odd jobs on the farm. My brothers and I didn't like him. He was surly. He never spoke to us, so we decided to hate him.

One afternoon we found his van parked by the sheds. He was nowhere to be seen. We guessed he'd be up at the house talking to our dad. So we threw some mud at the van. At first it was just a bit – at the wheels. Soon we got carried away and just hurled mud at the body of the van – on the sides, across the bonnet, even onto the roof. Not a word passed between us but an unspoken pact developed. We were going to cover the whole thing.

It didn't take more than about five minutes. Then we waited, crouched behind a pile of old apple boxes. My heart thumped. My hands stank. I felt the mud drying. I sat there in the long, damp grass and peeled mud off my skin.

My brothers tugged me down and hissed at me to be quiet. Mr Savage was coming. I peered through the wooden slats in one of the boxes. He had a pair of dark blue overalls. He stopped in front of the van and started cursing. He shouted for us. We froze.

When he left, we came out from behind the boxes. Hot and sweaty with mud that somehow had managed to smear on our faces.

'We look a right flippin' mess!' said Tom. We all laughed and ran then down the lane, whooping and yelling and then running hard and fast for the joy of it, gulping in the summer air.

My dad must have heard what happened but he never said anything. He hated Mr Savage too.

Dear Tom,

Last week we were evacuated to the countryside and I am writing to tell you all about it.

We had to line up in the playground at school in a long crocodile and Mrs Thomas stood at the front of the queue. She checked that everyone had their case, gas mask and label. Then we walked down to the railway station. Lots of mums came to wave goodbye. We stood around for ages and then boarded the train. We leaned out of the window and waved. Some of the little ones were crying and so too were the mums. Some tried to cling onto their children and one poor lady had to be held back and given a seat by a soldier. My mum wasn't able to come as she was working in the hospital and they were short-handed on account of the last night's bombing over Vauxhall.

The train journey seemed to last for ever, trundling through small towns, tiny stations and past fields and hills. I've never seen so much grass and so many cows and sheep. We ate our bread and an apple when Mrs Jenkins told us that we could.

At long last, we arrived at our destination. We all got off the train, lined up on the platform and Mr Thomas led the way to the village hall. You should have seen the hill we had to climb! Once there we had to stand up on the stage while people checked our names off. Then came the worst bit. The villagers walked up and down picking which ones to have.

Well, you can guess who got left to the last. Yes, you're right, Spud and myself. In the end an old bloke chose us and we went back to his cottage. It's not too bad really. We share a back room. You can imagine our eyes when we saw what Mrs Gardiner, that's their name, cooked for breakfast. We had porridge and then two slices of bacon each!!

I'll write more when something interesting happens. I hope you and Billy are OK.

Your old friend,

Cobber

Non-fiction models

Opening sets the scene – when, where and what	Dear Tom,

Dear Tom,

Last week we were evacuated to the countryside and I am writing to tell you all about it.

Use names

Leaving

We had to line up in the playground at school in a long crocodile and **Mrs Thomas** stood at the front of the queue. She checked that everyone had their **case, gas mask and label**. Then we walked down to the railway station. Lots of mums came to wave goodbye. We stood around for ages and then boarded the train. We leaned out of the window and waved. Some of the little ones were crying and so too were the mums. Some tried to cling onto their children and one poor lady had to be held back and given a seat by a soldier. My mum wasn't able to come as she was working in the hospital and they were short-handed on account of the last night's bombing over Vauxhall.

Use a few period details

Describing what happened

Personal details

On the train

The train journey seemed to last for ever, trundling through small towns, tiny stations and past fields and hills. **I've never seen so much grass and so many cows and sheep.** We ate our bread and an apple when Mrs Jenkins told us that we could.

Give writer's views

Arriving

At long last, we arrived at our destination. We all got off the train, lined up on the platform and Mr Thomas led the way to the village hall. **You should have seen the hill we had to climb!** Once there we had to stand up on the stage while people checked our names off. Then came the worst bit. The villagers walked up and down picking which ones to have.

Informally addressing the reader

Being chosen

Good news

Well, you can guess who got left to the last. Yes, you're right, Spud and myself. In the end **an old bloke** chose us and we went back to his cottage. It's not too bad really. We share a back room. You can imagine our eyes when we saw what Mrs Gardiner, that's their name, cooked for breakfast. We had porridge and then two slices of bacon each!!

Informal language

End note!

I'll write more when something interesting happens. I hope you and Billy are OK.

Your old friend,

Cobber

Dear Sir,

I am writing to inform you that the children from St Peter's Primary school in Vauxhall have all been evacuated to the village of Chalford in Gloucestershire.

In accordance with procedures set out by the Ministry, the children were first registered at the school. After that, they were carefully labelled so that no one could be lost. Then the whole school was marched, in a crocodile, down to the railway station.

Once they had reached the station, the school had to wait while the train from the West Country arrived. After it had been stoked with coal, the children were boarded. There were thankfully no scenes of distress that could not be dealt with. Next, the train made its way to Gloucestershire where it stopped near Stroud.

Following their arrival, the children were taken to the local village hall where a careful selection procedure took place, matching the children to families. By nightfall, they were billeted with villagers.

Tomorrow, the head teacher, Mrs Thomas, has taken responsibility for visiting the said children, in order to assure that the accommodation is clean and meets with current standards. Besides, it is unlikely that any assistance will be given where standards are not met.

In the future, all children are to attend the local school where Mrs Thomas and her assistant teacher, Mrs Jenkins, will both join the staff. Rationing will continue but only for all those who have children billeted with them. Ration books must be surrendered to those families.

Finally, villagers have been notified that children should not be used to work in the fields during school, as this has been a problem elsewhere.

Yours sincerely,

M. J. Grabbem

Billeting Officer

A Simple Card Trick

Have you ever watched TV and seen magicians performing card tricks? Have you ever wondered how they baffle the audience? Have you ever wanted to perform a trick yourself? Using cards for magical tricks has been around for over a thousand years. It is not all that difficult. If you are interested, then read on.

What you need: At least two people to trick, a pack of cards.

What the trick looks like: One of the people watching is asked to take a card from the pack and look at it without you seeing. Then they have to put the card back in any place they wish. You then spread out the cards and point to the one that they had chosen . . . as if by magic!

How the trick is done:

1. Before starting the trick, tell those watching that you had better check that all the cards are there.
2. Quickly flick through the pack and remember the card at the top.
3. Now put the pack on a table.
4. Next, ask someone to cut the pack, look at the bottom card (without you seeing) and remember it.
5. There are now two half-packs on the table.
6. After that, ask the volunteer to halve the middle pack again.
7. Now pick up the packs and put them all together.
8. When you do this make sure that pack with the bottom card that your volunteer memorised is placed on top of the original top card that you memorised.
9. At last, you can spread the cards out on the table.
10. The card that the volunteer chose will be to the left of the card that you first memorised.
11. Finally, hum and hah, as if letting the magic work, before revealing their card.

This is a simple enough trick. You will need to practise shuffling the decks quickly so that the people watching do not realise how it was done.

A Simple Card Trick

Opening – tries to interest the reader so they read on	Have you ever watched TV and seen magicians performing card tricks? Have you ever wondered how they baffle the audience? Have you ever wanted to perform a trick yourself? Using cards for magical tricks has been around for over a thousand years. It is not all that difficult. If you are interested, then read on.

Notice use of questions to interest the reader

What is needed

What you need: At least two people to trick, a pack of cards.

Often a list

Overview of intended result

What the trick looks like: One of the people watching is asked to take a card from the pack and look at it without you seeing. Then they have to put the card back in any place they wish. You then spread out the cards and point to the one that they had chosen . . . as if by magic!

How the trick is done:

Numbers used to help order steps

1. **Before** starting the trick, tell those watching that you had better check that all the cards are there.

Notice use of connectives to organise sequence

2. Quickly flick through the pack and remember the card at the top.
3. **Now** put the pack on a table.
4. **Next**, ask someone to cut the pack, look at the bottom card (without you seeing) and remember it.

What to do – in correct order, step by step

5. There are now two half-packs on the table.
6. **After that,** ask the volunteer to halve the middle pack again.
7. **Now** pick up the packs and put them all together.
8. **When** you do this make sure that pack with the bottom card that your volunteer memorised is placed on top of the original top card that you memorised.
9. **At last,** you can spread the cards out on the table.
10. The card that the volunteer chose will be to the left of the card that you first memorised.
11. **Finally**, hum and hah, as if letting the magic work, before revealing their card.

Final point

This is a simple enough trick. You will need to practise shuffling the decks quickly so that the people watching do not realise how it was done.

Another Simple Card Trick

If you have just learned how to perform one simple card trick – then you may well wish to learn another, more demanding one. Read on – and soon you too will be able to flabbergast your friends!

What you need: A few spectators and a pack of cards.

What the trick looks like: The pack is split in two. You take one half and a volunteer takes the other. Both of you choose one card from your respective packs. The packs are put together to make one pack again. Then you reveal the two cards, beside each other!

How the trick is done:

a. First, ask the volunteer to shuffle the cards and cut the pack in two.
b. Then, let the volunteer keep one half and give you the other.
c. Now, each of you should now shuffle your cards.
d. Explain to the volunteer that each of you should now choose a card, remove it and memorise it – without anyone seeing.
e. When you select your card, take a quick look at the bottom card in your pack.
f. You do not have to remember your chosen card at all.
g. Now both of you put your selected cards on the top of your own decks.
h. After that, ask the volunteer to place both packs on the table.
i. Next you put your pack on top of the volunteer's. This means that the card that was on the bottom of your pile is now next door to the volunteer's card.
j. Ask the volunteer to cut the whole pack once more.
k. Finally, end the trick by explaining that your card was (*give the name of the card that was at the bottom of your pack*).
l. Spread out the cards and, of course, the volunteer's card will be next to yours!

This is a simple but impressive trick. If you want to learn more magic tricks then try looking on the internet at some of the magic websites.

Pirates at Large!

Pirates are sea robbers. They have been around since we first began to trade and travel by ship.

Pirates attack ships at sea but will also attack ports. Their aim in life is to steal treasure so, usually, they attack merchant ships that are carrying goods.

Pirates can be found anywhere there are water and trading routes. In the past, pirates in the Mediterranean were called 'corsairs'. The 'buccaneers' who created havoc in the West Indies attacked treasure ships travelling back to Europe. There are still some modern pirates in the South China seas.

The film *Pirates of the Caribbean* showed buccaneers. Buccaneers originally came from Cuba, which at that time was known as Hispaniola. Many of them had been criminals or people without proper homes. They lived on the island off wild pigs that they roasted. However, in the 1630s the Spanish drove them out and slaughtered all the pigs. So the buccaneers stole ships and began to loot the Spanish merchant ships.

The buccaneers' first stronghold was a small island called Tortuga which had a sheltered harbour. It was in a good position because it was just off one of the main shipping routes. On the island, the buccaneers built a fort that had 24 cannons to protect the harbour.

Many people think that life as a pirate might have been fun but of course they were often very cruel. Conditions were not good and some lived a dreadful life. However, films and books still keep alive the idea that a few pirates were like Robin Hood, heroes of the seas!

Non-fiction models

Pirates at Large!

| Definition of subject – what it is | Pirates **are** sea robbers. They have been around since we first began to trade and travel by ship. | Reports are usually in the present tense |

| What they do | Pirates attack ships at sea but will also attack ports. Their aim in life is to steal treasure so, usually, they attack merchant ships that are carrying goods. |

| Where they are found – location | Pirates can be found anywhere there are water and trading routes. In the past, pirates in the Mediterranean were called 'corsairs'. The 'buccaneers' who created havoc in the West Indies attacked treasure ships travelling back to Europe. There are still some modern pirates in the South China seas. | Provide specific information such as place names |

| Information about buccaneers | **The film *Pirates of the Caribbean* showed buccaneers.** Buccaneers originally came from Cuba, which at that time was known as Hispaniola. Many of them had been criminals or people without proper homes. They lived on the island off wild pigs that they roasted. However, in the 1630s the Spanish drove them out and slaughtered all the pigs. So the buccaneers stole ships and began to loot the Spanish merchant ships. | Notice use of 'topic' sentences to introduce the subject of a paragraph |

| A buccaneer's stronghold | **The buccaneers' first stronghold was a small island called Tortuga** which had a sheltered harbour. It was in a good position because it was just off one of the main shipping routes. On the island, the buccaneers built a fort that had 24 cannons to protect the harbour. |

| End – tries to relate subject to reader | Many people think that life as a pirate might have been fun but of course they were often very cruel. Conditions were not good and some lived a dreadful life. However, films and books still keep alive the idea that a few pirates were like Robin Hood, heroes of the seas! |

Famous Buccaneer Pirates

Many of the bucanneers became famous and stories were told about them across the world.

Mary Read must have been fascinating because she was a female pirate! She left home to become a sailor, dressed to look like a man. However, her ship was captured by pirates, on the way to the West Indies. Mary joined the pirates but their ship was captured in turn by 'Calico Jack' Rackham and his wife Ann Bonny. Mary and Ann became great friends and the story is told of the pair of them fighting the British Navy fiercely while the rest of the crew hid below!

Another famous female pirate was Grace O'Malley. Because Grace cut her hair short to make her look like a man, her nickname was 'Baldy'. Grace had a whole fleet of small boats and ships that she kept off the coast of west Ireland. She lived in a small stone castle and used her 20 ships to attack merchant vessels. In 1593 she was granted a pardon by Queen Elizabeth so she gave up pirating. However, there wasn't much change because she just passed the business on to her sons!

One of the most successful pirates was known as Black Bart. Bartholomew Roberts captured over 400 ships in the 1720s. He was known as a daring, handsome captain and was even popular with his crew. He never drank any-thing stronger than tea! Many pirates shared the spoils of battle with the crew and decisions were made fairly, with every man taking a vote. Black Bart made his crew promise not to gamble or fight on ship. They were not allowed to burn a candle at night and anyone caught bringing a woman on board would be marooned.

The most frightening pirate of all had to be Blackbeard. Edward Teach wore six pistols and to make himself look fierce he tied his beard into plaits and adorned his hair with pink ribbons. This gave him a rather wild look. He was killed in 1718 by Robert Maynard who not only killed Blackbeard but then proceeded to behead him!

Famous pirates are still remembered in books, films and by word of mouth. Their reputations have lasted hundreds of years. Of course, if you met a pirate today it might not be so exciting. Perhaps they are best left to our imagina-tions.

How to Hide a Pirate's Treasure

The Caribbean has many thousands of tiny islands. Some have no one living on them at all. These made useful places for pirates to hide their treasure. The idea was that they would return at a later date to dig it up.

One famous pirate, William Kidd, said that he had buried an enormous treasure of £100,000 worth of gold and gems. Since then, not a stone or coin has been found! How do you think he managed to hide so much so secretly?

If I was asked to bury treasure, I would identify a place where no one could come across it by accident. This would mean finding a place where people did not often go so that no one could stumble across the loot. The sort of place that I would look for would be uninhabited, and also a hostile environment. Deserts, mountain ranges, icy wastes and beneath the sea would all be on my list because they are inaccessible to most people. Desert islands would also be ideal because there would be little chance of anyone discovering the treasure.

Once I had found the right place, I would then need a way of hiding or burying the treasure. It could be placed into a deep hole and covered with something hard like concrete so that it could not be dug up. Or I might hide it in a cave up a mountainside where it was impossible to climb without a lot of equipment.

It might be a good idea to disguise the treasure so that it looked ordinary. For instance, jewels could be covered in clay and be put in an old box so that they looked nothing like jewels at all.

Perhaps the best place to hide something would be below the sea. I would make a massive container out of heavy metal and concrete so that it would not move. I would place this in a deep part of the ocean where only a submarine can go. This would make it almost impossible for anyone to discover so the treasure would be safe. In order to recover it, I would ensure that only I had the co-ordinates!

Hiding treasure would be easy enough – if you had enough help and money to keep the secret well guarded!

How to Hide a Pirate's Treasure

The Caribbean has many thousands of tiny islands. Some have no one living on them at all. These made useful places for pirates to hide their treasure. The idea was that they would return at a later date to dig it up.

One famous pirate, William Kidd, said that he had buried an enormous treasure of £100,000 worth of gold and gems. Since then, not a stone or coin has been found! **How do you think he managed to hide so much so secretly?**

If I was asked to bury treasure, I would identify a place where no one could come across it by accident. This would mean finding a place where people did not often go **so that** no one could stumble across the loot. The sort of place that I would look for would be uninhabited, and also a hostile environment. Deserts, mountain ranges, icy wastes and beneath the sea would all be on my list **because** they are inaccessible to most people. Desert islands would also be ideal **because** there would be little chance of anyone discovering the treasure.

Once I had found the right place, I would then need a way of hiding or burying the treasure. It could be placed into a deep hole and covered with something hard like concrete **so that** it could not be dug up. Or I might hide it in a cave up a mountainside **where** it was impossible to climb without a lot of equipment.

It might be a good idea to disguise the treasure **so that** it looked ordinary. For instance, jewels could be covered in clay and be put in an old box **so that** they looked nothing like jewels at all.

Perhaps the best place to hide something would be below the sea. I would make a massive container out of heavy metal and concrete **so that** it would not move. I would place this in a deep part of the ocean **where** only a submarine can go. This would make it almost impossible for anyone to discover so the treasure would be safe. In order to recover it, I would ensure that only I had the co-ordinates!

Hiding treasure would be easy enough – if you had enough help and money to keep the secret well guarded!

Sidebar annotations:

Opening – introduces the need for the explanation

Use of question to set up the need for 'explanation'

Set of simple explanations showing cause and effect

Notice use of causal connectives ('so', 'because', 'this causes') plus information and ideas

End of summary points

How to Find Pirates' Treasure

The rewards for pirates could be great. For instance, in 1820 the *Mary Dear* landed on the Cocos Islands in the Pacific Ocean. There the crew buried 12,000 gems, seven treasure chests of golden ornaments and 9,000 gold coins. Having buried their loot they set fire to the ship and rowed off in longboats. However, when they reached land, they were all arrested. None of the crew could return to dig up their treasure because they were imprisoned. It has not been recovered since – though many have tried!

If I was called in to help discover pirate treasure in the Cocos Islands, I would have a number of ways to find the treasure.

First of all, I would identify all the places where the treasure might have been hidden. This would include sandy areas, caves, lakes and places where it might have been buried that are near to the shoreline. I would check that the shoreline had not changed so that we were not looking in the wrong place!

Next, I would use diggers to dredge up all the sand and sift it so that the grains fell back onto the sand and larger objects were retained. I would also use large magnets to help identify any metallic objects so that I could distinguish metal from other materials.

Also, I would have a team of workers using metal detectors criss-crossing other areas near the shoreline. Any sign of metal would cause the detectors to sound and identify where we needed to dig and explore further.

Finally, I would use sound waves to identify unusual objects lying below the surface because the pirates might have buried the treasure quite deep. This would also be needed because so much time has passed since the treasure was buried it could be under many layers of earth and silt.

I know that it is unlikely that I will be called in to search for pirate treasure because I am not famous for discovering much. In fact, the only discovery that I am known for was the time when our cat stole a chunk of Cheddar from the fridge and I found it hiding behind the kitchen door!

12 The Mews,
Gotham City,
Soupershire.

Dear Robin

I am writing to persuade you to give up your life with Batman and go back to school.

For the last few years, you have been trailing behind Batman, mopping up after his handiwork. He treats you like a second-class citizen and we think that you deserve better. Have you not noticed how he takes all the credit? Isn't it always Batman who barges in first, with you following behind? Surely you are worth more than this?

Also, I am concerned that you have been falling behind with your education studies. Last year your Level 3 in maths, English and science at the end of Key Stage 3 was not good at all! You may be able to fight like a tiger but there are no GCSEs in that! I know that your results in PE are good but in the other subjects you are not up to scratch.

If you do not perform well at GCSE then your hopes of a well-paid job are limited. It is all right for Batman. He is older than you and has had time to gather a fortune. What will you do when you are older?

Furthermore, have you thought about what would happen if you become seriously injured? Supposing the Joker managed to get his revenge? What then? I have been concerned for some time that Batman is becoming increasingly risky in his approach and is therefore putting you in danger.

Why not give up this life of hiding behind Batman's cape? Go back to school full-time and gain some good qualifications. Then you will have a good future. You are very welcome to stay with me.

Yours truly,

Cat Woman

Non-fiction models

12 The Mews,
Gotham City,
Soupershire.

Dear Robin

Introduces topic

I am writing to persuade you to give up your life with Batman and go back to school.

Series of attempts to persuade

For the last few years, you have been trailing behind Batman, mopping up after his handiwork. He treats you like a second-class citizen and we think that you deserve better. Have you not noticed how he takes all the credit? Isn't it always Batman who barges in first, with you following behind? Surely you are worth more than this?

> **What you are doing is demeaning**
> **Use of questions**

Also, I am concerned that you have been falling behind with your education studies. Last year your Level 3 in maths, English and science at the end of Key Stage 3 was not good at all! You may be able to fight like a tiger but there are no GCSEs in that! I know that your results in PE are good but in the other subjects you are not up to scratch.

> **Use of facts**

If you do not perform well at GCSE then your hopes of a well-paid job are limited. It is all right for Batman. He is older than you and has had time to gather a fortune. What will you do when you are older?

> **Your future may be in jeopardy**

Furthermore, have you thought about what would happen if you become seriously injured? Supposing the Joker managed to get his revenge? What then? I have been concerned for some time that Batman is becoming increasingly risky in his approach and is therefore putting you in danger.

> **Possibility of danger!**

Final attempt to persuade

Why not give up this life of hiding behind Batman's cape? Go back to school full-time and gain some good qualifications. Then you will have a good future. You are very welcome to stay with me.

Yours truly,

Cat woman

The Warren
Tangle Wood
Bunnishire

Dear Mr Wolf

I am writing to persuade you to give up your lifelong habit of eating meat and to become a vegetarian. I have a number of reasons for suggesting this.

First of all, you have been terrorising the warren and threatening the younger rabbits. We are no longer able to accept this sort of behaviour. Only last week several baby rabbits disappeared from the edge of the wood and it has been reported that you were sighted in the area! This sort of behaviour is causing much misery and we will no longer put up with it.

Also, a diet of meat is not good for your health. You are not eating any fruit or vegetables and therefore we have concerns about your figure. Have you noticed that you are beginning to put on the pounds through eating too much fatty meat? Your belly is dragging along the ground. Do you want to end up being known as the local roly-poly wolf? If you get too large, you will not be able to squeeze into your den at night!

As well as putting on weight, your diet may mean that you develop scurvy from a lack of vitamin C. This is of great concern, as the local animal hospital will not be pleased to have you on its ward. All the sick animals would be terrified!

Furthermore, you need to get more exercise. You have become lazy and spend too much time hanging round the warren waiting to pounce on a poor unsuspecting bunny. We recommend that you make daily visits to the gym and take up aerobics in order to lose weight.

Finally, we would like to recommend that you read *Becoming a Vegan, the Wolf Way* and stop eating rabbit meat. If you carry on attacking the local rabbits then we will have to report you to the wolf patrol force.

Yours truly

Old Bunny

Get rid of giants!

**Yes – that is what the *Daily Sun Spot* says.
And we know that all sensible people agree!
These ugly, savage brutes are not welcome
because they**

- tread on people
- eat sheep and cows
- break down walls
- uproot trees and magic beanstalks
- snore loudly and keep people awake.

Do you want these brutish savages in your
town? If not, sign our petition to get rid of
them – and win a free mystery prize!

Punchy and to-the-point headline

Get rid of giants!

Emotive description

So no one can disagree!

Yes – that is what the *Daily Sun Spot* says. And we know that <u>all sensible people agree!</u> These <u>ugly, savage brutes</u> are not welcome because they

List of negative points

- tread on people
- eat sheep and cows
- break down walls
- uproot trees and magic beanstalks
- snore loudly and keep people awake.

Question to which there is only one answer

Do you want these brutish savages in your town? If not, sign our petition to get rid of them – and <u>win a free mystery prize!</u>

A tempting extra

Dragons must go

The local council must work harder to rid the countryside of dragons. There have been too many examples locally of dragon-related incidents and this paper has decided to speak out.

Many have argued that dragons protect the area, reduce the number of princesses and are useful for guarding treasure. Some have even suggested that dragon flights should be increased as these are considered to be a popular method of travelling.

Popular maybe – but what about the flight to the icy north last year when the dragon became hungry and ate all the passengers? The local area has not been able to put in for the 'Best Kept Town' competition for the last twelve years due to scorched fields and hedges!

The council must relocate the dragons in an area acceptable to them but where they do not constitute a menace to the rest of us.

Phone in: If you agree or disagree – take part in our phone-in to see how many of the local population want to be rid of dragons. Dial 102938475 if you think YES. Dial 06574823902 if you think NO.

Visit us NOW
at the

Magic Bean Store

Attractions for all the family!

Be enchanted by our Magical Emporium. From the outside you will see a humble abode. But step in, and you will find a different world!

The indoor area extends for many miles, including: the wizard's restaurant; shops selling everything a spell master will need; toy corners for those special gifts; giant sandpit for restless giants; water zone for sprites; pet corner where you can watch bats and rats at play; and our world-famous dragon yard.

Visit the aMAZEing maze and lose unwanted members of your family for centuries.

- **Don't delay.**
- **Free tickets for first-time visitors.**
- **Lucky ticket numbers.**
- **Prizes for youngsters.**

Don't look daft with a wonky wand or a broom with no zip.
Buy from Wanda the wand maker!
Guaranteed speed – Brooms with zoom . . .

Moonday to Saturn'sday: Dawn to Starlight.

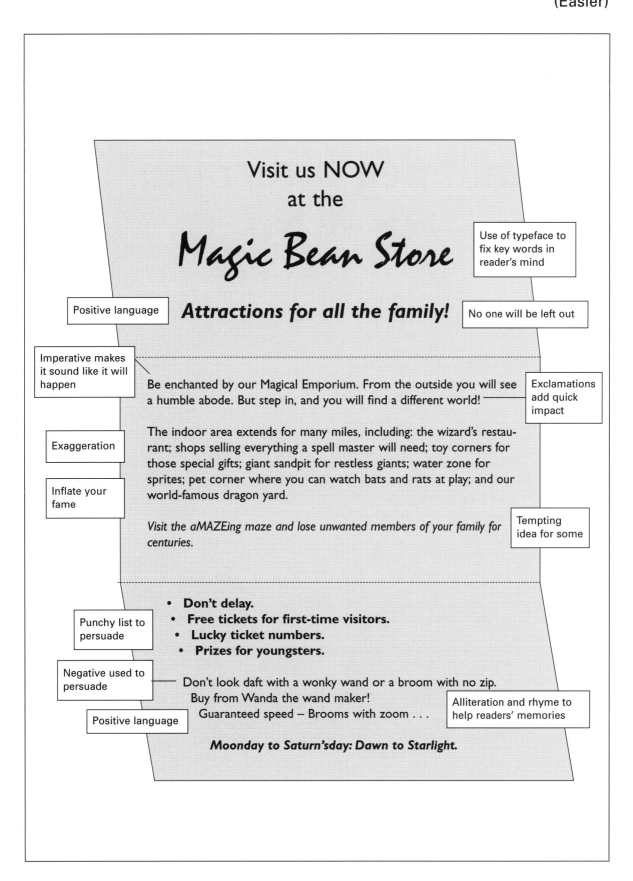

Visit us NOW
at the

Magic Bean Store

Attractions for all the family!

Use of typeface to fix key words in reader's mind

Positive language

No one will be left out

Imperative makes it sound like it will happen

Be enchanted by our Magical Emporium. From the outside you will see a humble abode. But step in, and you will find a different world!

Exclamations add quick impact

Exaggeration

The indoor area extends for many miles, including: the wizard's restaurant; shops selling everything a spell master will need; toy corners for those special gifts; giant sandpit for restless giants; water zone for sprites; pet corner where you can watch bats and rats at play; and our world-famous dragon yard.

Inflate your fame

Visit the aMAZEing maze and lose unwanted members of your family for centuries.

Tempting idea for some

- **Don't delay.**
- **Free tickets for first-time visitors.**
- **Lucky ticket numbers.**
- **Prizes for youngsters.**

Punchy list to persuade

Negative used to persuade

Don't look daft with a wonky wand or a broom with no zip.
Buy from Wanda the wand maker!
Guaranteed speed – Brooms with zoom . . .

Alliteration and rhyme to help readers' memories

Positive language

Moonday to Saturn'sday: Dawn to Starlight.

Ban

Chimney sweeping

by young boys
NOW

We demand an end to this inhuman practice

These young boys:

- are exploited by their masters
- earn the money
- but never get to spend it
- cannot read or write
- are unwashed
- are poorly clothed
- often go hungry
- have sores on their elbows and knees
- have red eyes
- and skin, engrained with soot

Do these children get any thanks? –
No – just a beating if they complain

Here in Britain in 1830, we may be one of the richest countries in the world but the poor need our protection.

Join Charles Kingsley and Lord Ashley in their proposals:
  * Children under 9 should not work in factories
  * Children aged 9–13 work no longer than eight hours a day
  * Women and children not to work underground in coal mines

While the wealthy sit by warm fires and sip a glass of port, there are children starving to death. We must fight this injustice.

Feed the Poor

I am writing to persuade you that the court should be more generous towards the poor.

First of all, it seems unfair that the court should eat so well while the poor make do on very little. Only last week the court consumed some 70 sheep, 30 pigs, 15 bucks, over a thousand chickens, 30 geese, 2,000 pigeons, plus a cartload of pheasants, over 2,000 eggs and 500 pounds of butter. While the court will have enjoyed their feasting, the poor had very little. They lived upon a few vegetables, a rabbit or two, roots, berries and the milk from a cow, if they were lucky.

Second, the court has good shelter. There is a roof over your head every night and a bed to lie upon. You have covers to keep you warm, and when the winter is cold, you can sleep in the great hall near to the fire. You have a dog to keep your feet warm. But what do the poor have? Many have no real shelter. Some have leaking roofs. Their huts are cold. Their clothes are too ragged and thin to keep out the wintry winds.

Third, it is unfair that the poor are often the ones who do all the work but receive no goods, while the court does very little work and yet seems to receive everything. This cannot be judged to be fair by any proper person.

The truth is that the court is lazy and greedy. How will our children's children judge us when they look back and see how unfairly we have lived our lives? How will we be judged in the eyes of God when it is obvious that we treat the poor not as human beings but no better than the donkey in the stable? Why, many of the dogs that lie around the court are better treated!

Finally, I think that all those of us who are intelligent and noble people will see that a more equal share would be right and proper.

William de Corbeau, 1550

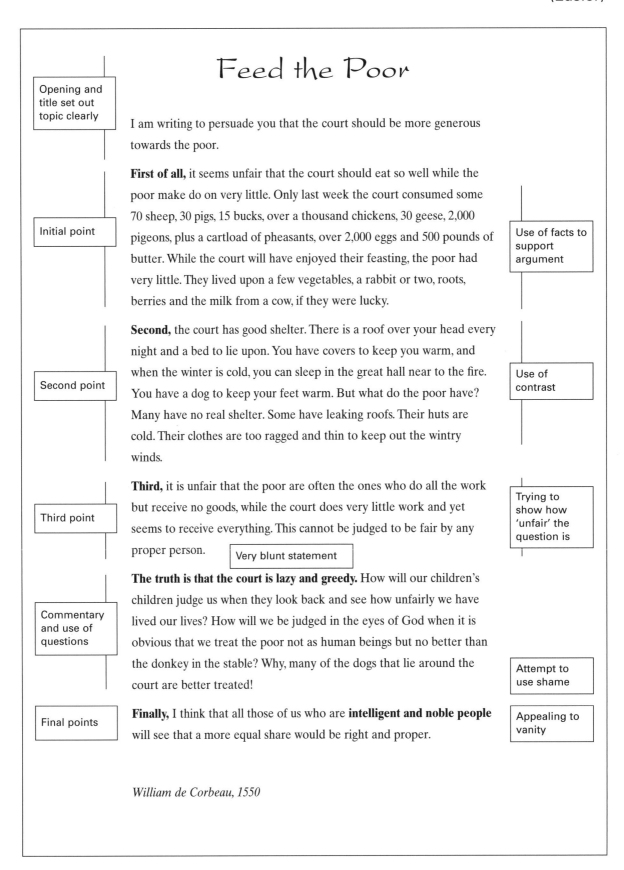

Feed the Poor

Opening and title set out topic clearly

I am writing to persuade you that the court should be more generous towards the poor.

Initial point

First of all, it seems unfair that the court should eat so well while the poor make do on very little. Only last week the court consumed some 70 sheep, 30 pigs, 15 bucks, over a thousand chickens, 30 geese, 2,000 pigeons, plus a cartload of pheasants, over 2,000 eggs and 500 pounds of butter. While the court will have enjoyed their feasting, the poor had very little. They lived upon a few vegetables, a rabbit or two, roots, berries and the milk from a cow, if they were lucky.

Use of facts to support argument

Second point

Second, the court has good shelter. There is a roof over your head every night and a bed to lie upon. You have covers to keep you warm, and when the winter is cold, you can sleep in the great hall near to the fire. You have a dog to keep your feet warm. But what do the poor have? Many have no real shelter. Some have leaking roofs. Their huts are cold. Their clothes are too ragged and thin to keep out the wintry winds.

Use of contrast

Third point

Third, it is unfair that the poor are often the ones who do all the work but receive no goods, while the court does very little work and yet seems to receive everything. This cannot be judged to be fair by any proper person.

Very blunt statement

Trying to show how 'unfair' the question is

Commentary and use of questions

The truth is that the court is lazy and greedy. How will our children's children judge us when they look back and see how unfairly we have lived our lives? How will we be judged in the eyes of God when it is obvious that we treat the poor not as human beings but no better than the donkey in the stable? Why, many of the dogs that lie around the court are better treated!

Attempt to use shame

Final points

Finally, I think that all those of us who are **intelligent and noble people** will see that a more equal share would be right and proper.

Appealing to vanity

William de Corbeau, 1550

Keep the Horse

I am writing to persuade you all that we should keep the offering that the cowardly Greeks have left us.

I propose that the wooden horse should be raised upon a great pedestal so that all Trojans may look upon it and remember how we protected our great city for ten years before the Greeks fled. It is obvious that they have left this as a token of their respect for our bravery. Surely, it would be churlish of us to ignore this offering in respect of our courage.

No one but a fool could ignore such a token. The truth is simple. We must raise this up on high so that we may never be forgotten. Future citizens will be able to see and remember our struggle.

Furthermore, such an offering could be made in the name of the gods. This will be made with due ceremony and accord so that the gods know that we are grateful for their blessing in saving the city and our kins-folk. It will stand in memory of all those who shed their blood in our name so that our children may live in a city free from Greek tyranny.

Some of you have suggested attacking the horse with spears. How will the gods behave if we attack this great offering to their mercy? Some of you have suggested casting this wooden horse from a high place so that it might be dashed upon the rocks, breaking into a thousand splinters. How will the gods react if we ignore them so?

Friends, we have fought side by side for ten long years for this moment. Let us take this gesture of respect from the Greeks and raise it on high to our gods. Let it be a monument to the fallen and a monument for the future. Let the wooden horse stand.

Teachers' notes

POETRY MODELS

Page 2: Poems conveying feelings, moods or reflections – ('A List of Small and Happy Things')

Reading
- Read through and discuss – which verse would they agree with? Underline any key words that are well chosen and add impact, e.g. 'shudder', 'boomerangs', 'catches'.
- Identify the pattern – repetition of 'How happy – when you . . .' and use of one sentence per verse.
- How should you read each verse, e.g. verse 3 loud, verse 5 rapidly?
- Try group performances.

Writing
- You could use the same theme or choose something different, e.g. How silent when, How angry when, How sad when, How joyful when, How amazing when, How wicked when . . .
- Make a list of possible ideas, e.g. more small and happy things – seeing the moon at night, rain after drought, finding an extra biscuit, a surprise present, seeing an owl at night, the pattern of frost on a window, finding a feather, taste of Marmite . . .
- Use the same pattern and turn ideas into simple verses. Try to use a well-chosen/slightly unusual word (especially the verbs) whenever possible, e.g. How happy – when you see the moon/imitating a silvery plate/on a dark cloth.

Pages 4–5: Poems conveying feelings, moods or reflections (Autobiography)

Reading
- Read through and discuss. Take initial responses – likes, dislikes, things that interest the children, similar experiences and so on.
- Build up clues – where did the writer live, what sort of early life did he have, what do we get to know about the writer?
- What is the impact of the choice of the word 'hot' to describe the darkness – what might the author have been thinking about?
- Highlight effective sections that build a picture plus strong use of language.

Writing
- Demonstrate how to write something similar by listing early memories of your own. Show the children how to take each idea and turn it into a line or two.
- Children should create a timeline for themselves, jot on events, memories, people, and places. Bringing in photos from home can add to this – as well as interviewing family or relatives about early events.
- Turn these into a similar poem.

Pages 6–9: Poems using metaphors and similies ('Images List' and 'Taking One Idea for a Walk')

Reading
- Read through the images list – ask the children to explain what the author is doing.
- In what way are windows like glass eyes or open mouths? Look at each mini-verse in the same way.
- Explain the difference between metaphor and simile: 'the windows are like glass eyes' is a simile: remove the word 'like' and you have a metaphor – 'the windows are glass eyes'.

Writing
- Look at the second poem to see how the poet has taken this idea and extended it: 'taken it for a walk'.
- If windows are eyes then they could stare, glare, weep, need rubbing and so on.
- You could continue this theme, writing extended metaphors as in the second poem – or use a different idea, e.g. windows/open mouths. In this case a window might – yawn, open, close, stick its tongue out, chatter, giggle, snigger, whisper . . . Open mouths/whispers silent words/as the night settles down/to sleep.

Page 10: Narrative poems ('The Blue Elephant')

Reading

- Read through and discuss:
  - What sort of person is the head teacher?
  - Why were Petie and the author excited?
  - Were they friendly with the Harrison twins – how do you know?
  - Why did the audience 'roar' – in what way?
  - Give two reasons why you think his father declared it 'a great success'.
  - Why did the Harrison twins not speak to them again?
  - Hot-seat Petie/a Harrison twin/Mr Weedler/his dad or mum about what happened.
  - Explain the poet's feelings and thoughts at the end.

Writing

- This sort of poem would be good to use alongside some of Michael Rosen's poems of everyday life.
- Discuss the sorts of memories that make good narrative poems in this vein – holiday events, sad times, funny things, getting in trouble and so on.
- Begin by children telling their anecdotes in pairs before writing.

Page 14: Narrative poems ('Left Behind')

Reading

- Read through and discuss:
  - Why were the different creatures left off the ark?
  - What other creatures got 'left behind'?
  - What does it mean at the end 'the storytellers' voices spoke/and a second ark appeared'? (The creatures were only saved in stories).

Writing

- This poem is built around a well-known story.
- Attempt retelling a well-known traditional tale as a narrative poem, e.g.

  > Once, not twice,
  > But once upon a time
  > Lived one, two, three little pigs
  > Who decided to seek their fortune?
  > In the big, wide world . . .

Pages 16–19: Performance poems ('Mysteries' and 'Cool!')

Reading

- Read the poems through and discuss:
  - Try answering some of the mysteries.
  - Decide on best ideas/lines.
  - Discuss the ending.
  - Read carefully through 'Cool!' and look for plays on words, e.g. 'hot under the collar' has two meanings – the shirt keeps me warm but also it makes me cross!

Writing

- 'Mysteries' is easy enough to imitate by copying the pattern.
- List ideas and turn them into new lines.
- Try to maintain the rhythm, e.g.

  > Why does the sun set in the west?
  > Why do show-offs think they're best?

- Once you have written one line, you will need to find a rhyme. With some words there are only a few rhymes. Try using *Black's Rhyming and Spelling Dictionary* (A. & C. Black).

Teachers' notes

- You could add on more 'cool' ideas or try a poem based around a similar word that has a new meaning, e.g. 'wicked'. Use a simple repeating frame such as 'somebody said/that xxxx was wicked/but I never . . .'
- List things which are considered to be 'wicked' and then turn each sentence around, e.g.

  Somebody said
  That my jeans were wicked
  But I never found them
  Being spiteful.

  Somebody said
  That peaches were wicked
  But I never saw them
  Exploding like a bomb.

FICTION MODELS

Pages 20–23: Story openings

Reading
- Read through and discuss:
  - What sort of story does each opening belong to – how do you know?
  - What clues are given about the characters or place?
  - Which opening would make you want to read on – put in order.
  - Categorise and label types of opening

Writing
- Imitate and invent new openings based on the 'types', e.g. 'Don't hang around by the car dump,' Mrs George said (warning opening).
- Children invent their own – swap books and check each other's.
- Share good starters.

Pages 24–27: Characterisation

Reading
- Read through and discuss:
  - What do we know about the characters in each example?
  - How does the writer achieve this?
  - Make a list of tactics the writer uses, e.g. description, clothing, use of an adverb, actions, dialogue, reactions of others, revealing thoughts and feelings, comments by other characters, using questions to make the reader think about a character.

Writing
- Imitate different tactics, sometimes copying the sentence structure, e.g.'I'm in pain!' whined Trev, holding out his hands to Courtney. (Imitation of number 5, page 24, showing use of powerful verb plus what character does as he speaks.)

Pages 28–31: New scene in a story

Reading
- Both the easier and harder examples are based on rewriting part of Chapter 8 from Michael Morpurgo's *The Sleeping Sword*. The main character, Bun (who has been blinded), is sent out to fetch his father in for tea from the potato field. (Because of theme, sensitive handling may be necessary.)
- How has the writer tried to show that Bun cannot see?
- Get the children to identify the structure used in both 'finding' stories – main character is asked to go somewhere, sets out, describe journey, finds/comes across something significant, ensuing event, ending.

Teachers' notes

Writing

- What else could Bun find/come across – list ideas.
- Plan with simple storyboard.
- Reset the same pattern by placing the main character into somewhere local or a place that the children know well.
- What does your character find? What happens as a result?

Pages 32–35: Story on a similar theme ('Dobber and the Silver Ring' and 'Tight as a Fist')

Reading

- Read through:
  - Both stories are 'finding stories'. Amy finds a ring, which brings her friendship. Brad finds a snake and his fear, which bring him back to his family.
  - Identify the basic pattern – opening reveals that main character has some negative attribute (lonely, angry, sad, jealous, bossy, etc.) – main character finds something – ensuing events help to solve initial problem.
  - Identify how writer is varying sentences to include adverb and '-ing' starts, short and long sentences, questions, tagging on '-ing' clauses.

Writing

- Decide on a character and setting.
- Then decide on negative attribute/aspect in their life.
- What will they find?
- How can this then help them to solve initial problem?

Pages 36–42: Opening scene from a play ('Humpty' and 'Sing a Song') plus Evaluation of playscript

Reading

- Perform script in small groups – listen and evaluate.
- Read evaluations on page 40 – identify useful phrases for writing own, e.g. 'The play script was successful because . . .'; 'For instance . . .'; 'The main strength was . . .'; 'If I was to criticise the play, I would say that . . .'; 'The weakest part . . .'; 'The best bit . . .'; 'We could have made it better . . .'
- How does the writer give clues about each character?
- What will happen next?

Writing

- Many nursery rhymes lend themselves to dramatisation. Because the plot is already well known it provides a simple structure for the children.
- Look at the conventions with the children.
- Before writing they should:
  - Decide how they will make each character distinctive.
  - Try role-playing the scene out in small groups before writing.
- Demonstrate how to turn a short role-play into a script. Remind them not to use too many stage directions.
- Playscripts should be performed. Using a tape recorder for rehearsal is a powerful way of helping children evaluate and improve.

Pages 43–45: Reading log entry

Reading

- These could be used in any term, as the children should be keeping reading logs for responding to their own reading as well as writing about their reading in class.
- Discuss the reader's reactions to what they are reading. These could be represented in a web or simple chart.

Writing

- Ask the children to identify sentence starters that will be useful for their own log entries, e.g. 'When we started reading, I thought . . .'; 'I hoped that . . .'; 'The writer made me feel . . .'; 'By . . .'; 'I like the way the author . . .'; 'The most frightening part . . .'; 'I did not like . . .'; 'It is strange that . . .'; 'My main prediction is that . . .'; 'This suggests to me . . .'; 'The main character is feeling . . . because . . .'; 'I know this because it says . . .'; 'My evaluation is that . . .'; 'My main concern is that . . .'; 'I am wondering if . . .'
- Model writing 'reading entries' for the children and read good examples out aloud.
- Encourage children to use a three-part paragraph:
  - Make a statement about the story (Tom is feeling afraid).
  - Support this with a quote (I know this because it says, 'He shivered, even though it was warm').
  - Add a further explanation (Tom is probably worried about the sounds that he can hear and is imagining what the enemy will do to him).
- Provide useful frameworks, e.g. write about your likes, dislikes, puzzles, patterns. Write about a character, using clues from the text. Write a school report for the main character. Draw a map of the setting. Write a 'Wanted' notice for the Baddie, etc.

Pages 46–51: Traditional tales ('Axe Soup' and 'Three Golden Peaches')

Reading

- 'Axe Soup' is a Russian variant of the 'Stone Soup', which the children may have heard of before. It is a simple trickster tale.
- Identify the pattern.
- Draw a simple story map of the story and use it for retelling in pairs and then story circles.
- 'Three Golden Peaches' is about a princess who nearly dies – because of the theme, sensitive handling may be necessary.
- Read and draw the story map.
- Look at the story pattern. There exists a problem – main character is given a task, main character wins through because of kindness.
- Identify story language, and motifs (e.g. three brothers, image of mountain, river, forest, magical fruit).
- What other stories have magical fruit in them (Adam and Eve, 'The Magician's Nephew' (C. S. Lewis).
- Draw main characters and attach clues about the sort of person they are – support ideas with quotes.

Writing

- A rewriting of 'Axe Soup' is on page 62 (Traditional tales – own version). This is simple enough, just alter who, where, the cooking utensils, the magical ingredient, what is being cooked, what is asked for.
- When writing own version, it is handy to have the original beside you so the pattern may be followed or altered.
- The end of 'Three Golden Peaches' suggests that there may be a sequel, if someone eats one of the golden, silver or copper peaches.
- It is helpful to draw a simple story map so that a journey could be central to what happens.
- Then decide on the task, e.g. either someone has to journey to fetch a peach or someone has to take a peach somewhere.
- Why are they after a peach?

Pages 52–54: Fables ('The Ants and the Grasshopper' and 'The Blacksmith and his Dog')

Reading

- Read both fables. What are the characteristics of a fable (about animals, short, provide a moral point)?
- The best-known fables are Aesop's. This is a large collection, almost exclusively they are moral/life message tales about animal behaviour – that tell us something about human behaviour.

Writing

- Ask the children to use the same pattern to write their own fable about a lazy creature.
- What creature might be lazy while others are busy?
- Write, with the original beside them, imitating the pattern but with some invention.

Teachers' notes

- On page 64 is a fable – own version, 'The Car Salesman and His Apprentice' which is based on the blacksmith story.
- Look for parallels, e.g. the rhythmic section.

Pages 55–57: Myths ('How Night Came' and 'Why the Robin has a Red Chest')

Reading
- 'How Night Came' is an African tale from Sierra Leone and the robin myth is Irish.
- A myth is a traditional tale that explains 'how' or 'why' something happens. Usually these are to do with the 'large' events – how the earth was made, how humankind began, why time runs forwards, why it thunders and so on. Many myths are rooted in a culture's religion.
- Note how some stories begin with a song or chant to tune in the listener.
- Look at the clues in the writing that show that this story was written for 'telling' ('Some say it was . . . but I don't know . . . you can imagine . . .').

Writing
- Agree on a potential 'how' or 'why' theme such as 'how thunder came'. Discuss ideas, e.g. a quarrel between giants, a greedy giant crying and moaning, etc.
- In pairs tell myth – try drawing a story map to fix the pattern.
- Retell, adding extra touches, such as a simile for description, short sentence at key moment, an adverb starter, and so on.

Pages 58–61: Legends ('The Legend of Randwick' and 'The Children of Hamelin')

Reading
- Legends are traditional tales that have some basis in fact. The first is a local legend about how a village's name arose. The second is more typical of a legend in that there may well have been a factual basis for the story.
- Provide children with the following information about Hamelin:
  - The Street of Silence in Hamelin is where the children are supposed to have left the town. Nowadays, dancing or music is forbidden.
  - Poppenberg Mountain has a cross made of stones beside it.
  - On the town hall is this inscription:
      In the year 1284 AD
      130 children born in Hamelin
      were led out of our town
      by a piper and lost in the mountain.
  - A children's crusade happened in 1212, as well as a plague, probably caused by rats in 1284.
  - Professional recruiters visited Hamelin between 1250 and 1285; they convinced many young people to move to the east.
  - Why did these young people leave?
  - Did people in the town invent the story to cover up what really happened?
- Discuss which they think is more of an 'oral' retelling – closer to speech as if someone was telling the tale. What are the clues?
- Prepare a retelling of either – reduce the story to a map or a 'bare bones'/skeleton – just a list of prompt words on a card.
- Create as a storyboard.
- Retell in pairs or small circles.
- Tell onto a tape and provide a tape of legends for another class.

Writing
- Either write a retelling of the Pied Piper or invent a local legend to explain the name of a local place.
- Build up to the writing through drawing, retelling orally and listing specific sentences and structures, e.g. similes, adverb starters, '-ing' starters, etc., that can be slotted into the written version.

Pages 62–65: Traditional tales, own versions ('Nail Stew' and 'The Car Salesman and His Apprentice')

Reading
- Read these two plus the originals on pages 46 and 54.
- Discuss changes and identify the basic pattern, looking for similarities.

Writing
- Create own versions by making similar alterations to the basic patterns.

Pages 66–68: Writing from another character's view

Reading
- Read these two together. They are both based on the scene in Betsy Byars' novel *The Midnight Fox* where Tom has just released the baby fox in Chapter 17, 'The Stormy Rescue'.
- They are good examples for showing the same event but through the eyes of two different characters.
- Discuss how the author reveals the character of Aunt Millie and Uncle Fred – look for details and discuss what it infers, e.g. 'her thin cotton robe' suggests that it is worn and maybe they are poor.

Writing
- Now take a scene – you only need something brief, avoid being too complicated – in which there are several characters who may well be seeing things differently. This usually works well where you have a child and an adult.
- To prepare for writing – hot-seat, or interview as journalists, the characters about the events.
- Then write in role.

Pages 69–74: New chapter in style of author

Reading
- Read these two 'warning' stories through. They are new chapters for *The Midnight Fox*.
- In the easier version, identify the pattern of the tale: warning opening ('be home on time') – walking somewhere – find something – play with it – remember warning – dash home – too late!
- In the harder version, identify pattern: warning opening about a place – go to the place – disaster – rescue – make way home.
- Look for sentence techniques such as adverb starters, '-ing' starters and powerful verbs.

Writing
- Create own new chapters based on your current novel.
- These could use the same 'warning' pattern. Remember to keep the chapter simple, like a short story itself.
- Build up to the writing through:
  - Hot-seating the character about the 'warning' event.
  - Story mapping or boarding to shape the plot.
  - Inventing specific sentence structures that could be used in the story.

NON-FICTION MODELS

Pages 75–78: Recounts (extracts from the 'Ugly Sister's Letters', 'The Green Van', Recount to a friend and recount to an unknown person)

Reading
- In all pieces, note structure (opening to introduce who, where, what, followed by events in chronological order, ending that comments) and language features (past tense, details to bring events alive, comments on what happened, use of temporal connectives such as 'before', 'first', 'next', 'later', to organise sequence).

Teachers' notes

- 'Ugly Sisters' (imagined recount): how does the writer bring the character alive?
- 'The Green Van' (real event): role-play Mr Savage phoning up the dad.
- 'Dear Tom': what details does the writer use to suggest this was from another time?
- 'Dear Sir': in what ways does the writing suggest that the two people do not know each other?

Writing
- Build up a list of temporal connectives that could be used to help organise a recount.
- Possible starting points for writing include:
  - Recount based on traditional tale, e.g. Jack's diary (retell original tale and then hot-seat main character).
  - Recount based on real anecdote (tell anecdotes in pairs and circles).
  - Historical recount – based on period being studied (list specific historical detail that might be included – role-play an event).

Pages 81–83: Instructions (Simple card tricks)

Reading
- Read and see if the children can follow either set of instructions; what else would help? (Diagrams or photos to show what is happening.)
- Tease out basic features – structure and organisation.
- Identify language features such as temporal connectives, use of question to draw reader in, etc.

Writing
- Let children create their own writing frame to help them write a set of instructions. As a topic, choose something that they know about, e.g. playing a game.

Pages 84–86: Non-chronological reports ('Pirates at Large!' and 'Famous Buccaneer Pirates')

Reading
- Read each through.
- Make a chart and extract basic information.
- Give each paragraph a heading and illustrate to create a mini-booklet about pirates.
- Identify how opening paragraph introduces the topic – subsequent paragraphs add information that is organised into sections (paragraphs) and not scattered wildly, ending with a summary comment or observation.

Writing
- Let children create their own writing frame for a report on a topic that really interests them – extreme sport, bungee jumping, keeping bees, aliens, UFOs . . .
- They should bullet-point and organise their information into boxes to avoid muddling paragraph content.
- Reports could be presented on a school website, as an e-mail attachment for another school or turned into mini-information booklets for a library.

Pages 87–89: Explanations ('How to Hide a Pirate's Treasure' and 'How to Find Pirates' Treasure')

Reading
- Read and discuss.
- Identify the key words needed to explain something (cause and effect), e.g. 'If . . .'; 'Because . . .'; 'So that . . .'; 'Would cause . . .'
- Check the basic pattern of the text: introduce the subject; explain in steps 'how' or 'why', and summarise or comment at the end.

Teachers' notes

Writing
- You need something to explain, and this is best kept for either a scientific or technological link. Occasionally, geography offers a topic such as the rain cycle or how a volcano works.
- Drawing the sequence of an explanation can be a simple way to prepare for writing.

Pages 90–92: Persuasive letters

Reading
- Read through and discuss.
- What is the point of view of the writer/the recipient?
- How does the writer try to persuade – list specific words/phrases and techniques, e.g. use of questions, 'If you do not . . . then your hopes will be dashed', etc.
- Identify structure, e.g. set out topic, use a number of persuasive arguments, summarise at end.

Writing
- Oral persuasion in pairs as a role-play would make a useful precursor to writing.
- You could use a superhero theme (persuade Superman to spend more time at the newspaper office) or a traditional tale (persuade the Ugly Sisters to let Cinderella go to the ball).

Pages 93–95: Persuasive news editorials

Reading
- Read both editorials. How do they differ?
- What sort of paper do they come from – how did you know?
- List similarities and differences.
- Identify persuasive devices, e.g. 'All sensible people agree . . .'; use of bullet points; use of questions; offer of free prize, etc.

Writing
- Let children prepare a half-minute broadcast (like a political party) to persuade the rest of the class. These could be presented and voted upon.
- Draw children's attention to use of language and keep listing devices and sentence structures that are handy.
- Choose simple topics such as: Get Rid of Wolves; Ban Foxes; Free Magic Beans for All; Release Rapunzel; Be Kind to Ugly Sisters; Seven Dwarfs for Post in Government; Hansel's Father Must Stand Trial, etc.

Pages 96–98: Persuasive leaflets

Reading
- Compare the two leaflets.
- Identify persuasive devices, e.g. exaggeration, exhortation, negatives (don't look daft), guarantees, use of facts, strong statements, e.g. 'We must . . .'

Writing
- Create own versions in a similar vein, adding illustrations.
- Use real leaflets and lift useful phrases and techniques.
- Imaginary subject, e.g. magical theme park.
- Historical topic, e.g. school for all (Victorians).

Pages 99–101: Persuasive arguments ('Feed the Poor' and 'Keep the Horse')

Reading
- Both of these examples are linked to history.
- Identify the structure and any useful language features such as: 'I propose . . .'; 'First of all . . . , secondly . . . , thirdly . . .'; 'The truth is . . .'; 'Furthermore . . .'; 'Finally . . .'
- Discuss use of counter arguments in the harder version, identifying what the counter argument might be and knocking it down.

Teachers' notes

Writing
- Identify a historical topic that migh   asons. Organise these into a framework – simple bo
- Write an opening and ending then p

DATE DUE

Demco, Inc. 38-293

112